HANDFASTING
A PRACTICAL GUIDE

Anna Franklin

First Published by Llewellyn Worldwide as
A Romantic Guide to Handfasting.
This revised edition published in 2009 by Lear Books

Lear Books
Windrush House
High Tor West
Earl Shilton
Leicestershire
LE9 7DN
England

Printed by Booksprint

Cover illustration © Paul Mason
Cover design Paul Mason

ISBN 978-0-9547534-9-8

Lear Books
www.learbooks.co.uk

Contents

3 Introduction

7 Chapter 1- The Historical Background

10 Chapter 2 – Organising the Handfasting
14 The Commitment

16 Chapter 3 – The Rituals
16 The Circle
19 Casting the Circle
20 Dissolving the Circle
21 A Pagan Handfasting Ceremony
24 A Wiccan Handfasting Ceremony
28 An Alternative Handfasting Ceremony
29 Legal Handfasting in the UK
30 The Great Rite
31 Renewing the Vows

32 Chapter 4 – Gods and Goddesses
32 The Bride and the Goddess
33 The Groom and the God
33 Goddesses of Love
39 Gods of Love

44 Chapter 5 - Gay Handfastings
44 Themes for Gay and Lesbian Handfastings
49 Lesbian Unions
49 Deities for Gay and Lesbian Handfastings
52 Herb Craft

53 Chapter 6 – Choosing the Moment
53 Phases of the Moon
55 The Sabbats
56 The Months
57 The Days of the Week

59 Chapter 7 – Handfasting Themes

70 Chapter 8 – Handfasting Customs
70 Tying the Knot
70 Jumping the Broom

72 Jumping the Cauldron
74 Sharing a Cup
74 Throwing the Bouquet
74 Confetti
75 Shoes
75 The Honeymoon
75 The Cake
78 The Hen Night
78 The Stag Night

79 Chapter 9 – What to Wear
80 Colour Magic
82 The Cord
83 The Ring

90 Chapter 10 – Herb Craft
90 The Language of Flowers
99 Plant Magic
109 Incense
114 Magical Oils
116 Bath Salts

117 Chapter 11 – The Feast
118 Savoury Dishes
120 Sweet Dishes
129 Wines and Ales

134 Chapter 12 – Spells and Charms

139 Chapter 13 – Handparting

141 Appendix 1 – Poems and Blessings

147 Appendix 2 – Anniversaries

149 Resources

INTRODUCTION

A handfasting is a Pagan wedding, usually the union of two individuals, perhaps two members of a coven or solo practitioners who meet and fall in love. It is the marriage rite used today by many Pagans, Druids, Heathens, Witches and Wiccans. During the ceremony, the couple declare their love and commitment to each other, and promise that they will live together for a year and a day or *'for as long as love shall last'* in the words of one ritual. At the end of that time, they may renew their vows, make a more permanent commitment and a legal marriage, or go their separate ways. In an age when, for whatever reason, many relationships do not last a lifetime and divorce is commonplace, it is perhaps a sensible option.

This might seem to be a very modern concept but the idea of a trial marriage – usually for a year and a day – is very old. In the south of England in Dorset there is a cliff called Handfast Point where, presumably, many such unions were made. The ancient and Mediaeval Irish would undertake trial marriages, clasping hands through a holed stone. If the couple got on, they would make more permanent vows; if not, they would go back to the stone and each walk off in a different direction. Some think that this is where the origin of the term handfasting originates; others think it may come from the custom of shaking hands over a contract. Then too, in some cultures, the hands of the bride and groom are bound together, and some Pagans adopt this practice as part of the handfasting ceremony.

Many Pagans think that it is very important for them to be able to declare their commitment to each other in a ritual that expresses their own beliefs, feeling that a secular ceremony is not as fulfilling and meaningful as the declaration of love before their Gods and their peers. The vows are usually written by the couple themselves to express their own needs and emotions. The handfasting is generally celebrated inside a magic circle, something that Pagans believe to exist 'between the worlds', i.e., neither wholly in the mundane world of humankind, nor wholly in the Otherworld of gods and spirits, but partly in both.

What happens in the circle affects not only this world, but also the Otherworld. The circle stands at the intersection of the worlds for the time it is invoked, momentarily at the centre of the Universe, ritually re-enacting the great cosmic theme of the love of the Goddess and the God and the eternal verity of human love, recreated and renewed with every lover that exists or ever existed. The pair enter as two separate people, and are transformed into a declared couple, a life changing event and an important rite of passage in life's journey.

The handfasting vows are believed, literally, to be taken before the Gods, and are therefore very solemn and binding. The coven or grove act as witnesses, sometimes with friends and family present (if they would like to be) with the ritual presided over by a priest or priestess, druid, clan chieftain or shaman. The couple exchange vows, promising to love and honour each other, and may give each other rings, have their hands loosely tied with coloured cords or ribbons, jump over the cauldron or broomstick, and share wine together. Afterwards there are the usual congratulations, the throwing of confetti, flower petals or rice, posing for photographs and a picnic or party.

The handfasting may be followed by a civil wedding, or in Britain, if it takes place in a venue sanctified for marriage in front of a registrar and contains certain wordage, it may constitute a legal marriage. At the time of writing, handfasting has no legal validity in most states of the USA and other parts of the world. Some Pagans hope that this will change with time as the Pagan religion becomes more accepted by the wider world. More traditional Pagans think that this kind of trial marriage only needs to be recognised by family and clan, and that giving it a legal status would negate the purpose of a trial marriage. Over the years, the fundamental idea of the handfasting has changed amongst some Pagan groups, and the initial idea of a trial marriage of a year and a day has given way to the permanent vows of a conventional marriage.

Please note that the handfasting rite may be used by heterosexual couples or partners of the same sex. It may even be adapted to encompass group marriages. The ideas in this book are only a starting point for your ceremony. Feel free to modify and change them to your needs, to write your own rituals and vows. The day is yours, so you can shape it the way you want.

Chapter 1
THE HISTORICAL BACKGROUND

Contrary to popular belief, marriages in the old days did not always take place with the benefit of clergy. Often only the rich could afford a church ceremony (which took place in the porch of the church, not inside), and in any case, in some areas, priests were thin on the ground, and one could not be found to conduct every marriage. In most parts of Europe a declaration before witnesses was enough to constitute a legal marriage, recognised by Roman Catholic Canon Law. Even children were married in this manner, with the consummation sometimes taking place years later. It wasn't until 1563 that the Council of Trent changed the law, and a priest and marriage ceremony were required to constitute a valid marriage in Catholic countries.

ROMAN COMMON LAW MARRIAGES
The ancient Romans could celebrate marriage *ex usu* by which if a woman, with the consent of her parents or guardians, lived with a man for a year without being absent for three nights, she became his wife. This custom was obsolete in Roman law by the time of the Republic.

ENGLISH HANDFASTINGS
The term 'handfasting' originates in the Anglo-Saxon word *handfæstung*, which meant the shaking of hands to seal a contract. A similar word exists in German and Danish. Among other things, it was applied to the act of betrothal in both England and Scotland. This betrothal itself was called, in Anglo-Saxon, a *beweddung* because the future husband was called upon to make a down payment, or *wed*, against the bride price of his lady. (This is the origin of our term 'wedding'.) The contract was sealed with a handshake or *handfæstung*.

IRISH HANDFASTINGS
In ancient Ireland, Teltown Marriages were temporary unions entered into at Lughnasa, the festival celebrated at the beginning of August. At Larganeeny

(*Lag an Aonaigh* "the hollow of the fair") there was an oral tradition, recorded in the nineteenth century, that a form of marriage was held there in Pagan times. A number of young men going into a hollow to the north side of the wall and an equal number of marriageable young women went to the south side of the wall, which was so high as to prevent them from seeing the men. One of the women put her hand through the hole in the gate, and a man took hold of it from the other side, being guided in his choice only by the appearance of the hand. The two who thus joined hands by blind chance were obliged to live together for a year and a day. At the end of that time they appeared together at the Rath (Fort) of Teltown and if they were not satisfied they obtained a deed of separation, and were entitled to go to Larganeeny again to get a new partner. If they were satisfied, a longer term arrangement was entered into.

One of the largest Lammas (i.e. Lughnasa) fairs was held at Kirkwall in the Orkney Islands off the coast of Scotland. The fair lasted eleven days and taking a sexual partner for its duration was a common practice. Such couples were known as 'Lammas brothers and sisters'. For couples thinking of a slightly longer term commitment this was a traditional time for handfasting. Couples would join hands through a holed stone, such as the ancient Stone of Odin at Stenness, and plight their troth for a year and a day. Many such temporary unions became permanent arrangements. The handfasting ritual was just one of the forms of marriages permitted under the ancient Brehon law. The same law declared how the property would be divided if the couple spilt, and how any children of the marriage would be cared for.

It wasn't until the middle of the nineteenth century that the registration of marriages was required by the government in Ireland

SCOTTISH HANDFASTINGS

In Scotland, the civil authorities recognised marriages constituted in the old style - consent to marry followed by intercourse at some later date - though the Scottish church did not. Such marriages were legal until 1940. As a result many English couples whose parents objected to their marriages crossed to the Scottish border town of Gretna Green where they could perform their own handfastings before witnesses. In Scotland the term handfasting or handfisting meant the shaking of hands to seal a contract, this might be a contract of employment, or a betrothal.

In 1820, the famous Scottish novelist Sir Walter Scott wrote of handfasting as a trial marriage in *The Monastery*:

> *"When we are handfasted, as we term it, we are man and wife for a year and a day; that space gone by, each may choose another mate, or, at their pleasure, may call the priest to marry them for life; and this we call handfasting."*

The practice was also mentioned by Thomas Pennant[1] recounting his tour of Scotland in 1772:

"Among the various customs now obsolete the most curious was that of handfisting, in use about a century past. In the upper part of Eskdale ... there was an annual fair where multitudes of each sex repaired. The unmarried looked out for mates, made their engagements by joining hands, or by handfisting, went off in pairs, cohabited until the next annual return of the fair, appeared there again and then were at liberty to declare their approbation or dislike of each other. If each party continued constant, the handfisting was renewed for life."

This account was confirmed in *The Old Statistical Account of Scotland*[2]

"At that fair (in Eskdale), it was the custom for the unmarried persons of both sexes to choose a companion, according to their liking, with whom they were to live till that time next year. This was called hand-fasting, or hand in fist. If they were pleased with each other at that time, then they continued together for life; if not, they separated, and were free to make another choice as at the first. The fruit of their connexion (if there were any) was always attached to the disaffected person. In later times...a priest... came from time to time to confirm the marriages."

WELSH BROOM JUMPING WEDDINGS

There was a custom of jumping the broom as a declaration of marriage in both Wales and England. As a child I remember an old lady saying that a couple were "living over the brush" meaning that a couple were living together without being legally married, but had a common-law relationship obtained by jumping over a broom. In Wales this was called the *priodas coes ysgub*, or broom-stick wedding.[3]

In Wales a broom was placed on the doorstep with its handle leaning on the door frame, and the couple had to jump over it in front of witnesses. The couple were free to part within the first year, and simply had to jump over the broom again. If a child had come, the man was obliged to support it. In Caernarvonshire the practice was overseen by the oldest man in the village and the broom was constructed of oak branches and called *ysgub dderwydd* or "druid's besom" indicating that the custom may have been very old indeed, dating back to the time of the Druids.

---

1   Thomas Pennant in his *Tour in Scotland* (London, 1790)
2   *The Old Statistical Account of Scotland* (1791-99)
3   "Welsh Folklore" by T. Gwynn Jones, Methuen and Co., London: 1930

Chapter 2
ORGANISING YOUR HANDFASTING

When you and your partner decide to become handfasted, there are a number of things to consider. Below is a checklist for organising a handfasting ceremony, and a few things to think about along the way. Each point will be covered in greater detail later in the book.

- Firstly (and very importantly) decide how much money you have to spend on the handfasting, and budget accordingly.
- Decide the date: you might like to consider the phases of the moon, 'lucky' days and so on.
- Decide on the style or theme of wedding (plain Pagan, Greek, Celtic, formal Wiccan, Mediaeval etc.)
- Draw up the guest list: decide on who you want to be present at the handfasting, whether you want to invite just the coven or non-Pagan friends and relatives too.
- Chose the site for the ceremony (indoors or outdoors) make your booking or get any relevant permissions
- Decide on the costumes or robes and who will wear them, and who will be responsible for paying for and supplying them.
- Who will officiate? A nominated celebrant should usually be in charge. This might be your high priest or priestess, druid, shaman, clan leader or friend. You might need to request a priest and priestess from a Pagan organisation
- Decide on the ritual and talk this over with the celebrant.
- Decide on the type of commitment you wish to make to each other, whether it is for a year and a day or for longer.
- Write your vows.
- Decide which gods and goddesses you want to call on to bless the ceremony. Don't mix traditions.
- Do you want to include the jumping of the broom or cauldron? Decide

on any customs you want to be part of the event, and where they will ft into the ceremony.

- Decide on an order or service, write it down, and let everyone who will be attending have a copy.
- If you having a legal civil ceremony, this will need to be co-ordinated with the ritual. Check out the legalities of handfasting in your area.
- Make sure that you let guests know what will be happening, what they will need to bring, and what they will need to do.
- Organise the flowers, garlands, chaplets and bouquets.
- Make the incense and anointing oils (if used), get a friend to make them, or purchase them if necessary.
- You might like to give the guests small gifts, such as a little posy or lucky charm.
- If you want to exchange rings you will need to buy these or have them made. Do you want them inscribed?
- Do you want music at the handfasting or the party afterwards? You might like to use live music suitable to the theme, or allow the coven bards and minstrels to perform. Alternatively you might use recorded music and will need to organise a sound system to play this on.
- You might like to have a handfasting certificate, signed by the celebrant. Some priests and priestesses supply these, or you could design one on a computer, print it, and ask the celebrant to sign it.
- Buy or make the cords that you will use to bind the hands.
- Decide on how you will decorate the circle, where you will place the altar and how you will dress it and so on.
- Decide whether you want an after-ritual party or picnic and book the venue.
- Organise the catering.
- Design and send your invitations telling people the time, date, and venue, describing what they might need to wear or bring.
- How will you and the guests get to the venue? Do you need to arrange transport for everyone?
- Would you like photographs of the event? You could employ a photographer, or just encourage friends to take pictures and let you have copies.
- Will you be going on a honeymoon afterwards? This needs to be booked and transport arranged
- Don't forget to send out thank you notes to everyone who helped you achieve your perfect handfasting.

BUDGETING FOR THE HANDFASTING:

You can see from the above checklist that there will be a number of expenses incurred in organising a handfasting. The event can be as simple or as lavish as you wish or can afford. You can have a beautiful simple ritual attended by friends and relatives and a plain picnic afterwards. Or you can have everyone dressed in mediaeval costume serenaded by minstrels followed by a banquet, but this will be expensive! Take into account the cost of flowers, food, transport, clothes, rings, cords, incense, and entertainment and so on. If you are not careful you might be horrified by a big bill when you get back from honeymoon, and this is not a good start.

THE CELEBRANT:

Though you and your partner can simply exchange vows in front of witnesses, it is more usual to have a celebrant preside over the ritual. If you belong to a coven this might be your high priestess or high priest, or both acting together. If you belong to a druid grove, the chief druid will probably be happy to perform the ceremony. Alternatively, you might ask the head of your Pagan clan, the local shaman, or simply a Pagan friend whom you trust. If necessary, you could apply to a Pagan organisation such as The Pagan Federation to put you in touch with a priest or priestess to help you. Some useful addresses can be found in Appendix 5.

THE GROOMSMAN

It is the custom for the groom to be attended by a groomsman. Long ago, it was the practice among some Germanic tribes to kidnap women from a nearby village to marry. Rather than undertake the enterprise alone, a man would take his best friend to help him. This is probably the origin of the 'best man' role. He was also called the bridesman or brideknight, and in more troubled times it was part of his duty to safeguard the wedding party. One of the reasons the bride stands to the left of the groom is so that his sword arm is free to protect her.

THE BRIDESMAID

The bride is attended by a married woman, called the matron of honour, and by young unmarried girls called bridesmaids. In the past, they all dressed the same and were veiled, and the groom was faced with the challenge of having to pick out his bride from the throng. As recently as Victorian times, the bridesmaids wore veils and dressed in white, like the bride.

Another reason the bridesmaids dressed like the bride was to confuse evil spirits who might try to spoil the wedding. This way, they wouldn't know who to choose!

12

FAMILY AND FRIENDS

As well as the coven or grove, it is natural to want to share your special day with family and friends, even if they are not Pagan. If you think they would be happy to attend, invite them along, but do not insist. Not everyone is yet comfortable with attending a Pagan ceremony. To reassure them you should let them know everything that will happen on the day, and explain the reasons behind each ritual act. They may like to watch from outside the circle, or if your celebrant is okay with the idea, then they might enjoy the experience of being part of the circle.

THE VENUE

Ideally, every Pagan would like to be married outdoors in some beauty spot, preferably an ancient stone circle. However, this is not possible in all cases, and you could consider woods, the seashore or secluded parkland. Wherever you hold rituals outside, you need to be sure that it is private, and that you obtain any relevant permissions.

Maybe you would rather not risk the weather and would like to be handfasted at home, or if you do not have the space, in a hired hall, hotel or community centre. Again, be sure that the proprietors are comfortable with what you are going to do and know what to expect.

If at all possible, decorate the site with greenery, flowers and coloured ribbons. You might like to outline the circle with flowers or crystals on this occasion. If the site permits, you could follow the mediaeval custom of strewing the floor with scented herbs: rosemary for constancy; lemon balm for joy; mint for clarity and so on.

THE RECEPTION

This may take place at the same site as the handfasting, or the party might adjourn to a hall or hotel after an outdoor handfasting. If possible decorate the hall with garlands of greenery, ivy and flowers. Wild flowers are particularly charming and have more significance than bought flowers - they are cheaper too. Include decorations associated with fertility and plenty, including wheat, fruit and nuts. These can be made into table decorations and centrepieces.

Sweets symbolise sweetness in the relationship, and are traditional in many cultures. They can be placed in dishes at intervals along the buffet, or gilded and scattered artistically along the tables. Decorate the place settings or buffet with sprigs of herbs, and twine some into the napkin rings.

Ask if you can make a shrine for images of the God and Goddess. Place them on a decorated cloth and arrange offerings of flowers and fruit before them. You might make paper hangings of suns, moons, stars and pentacles.

For the duration of the feast, the bride and groom may be placed on chairs or thrones of honour, beneath a canopy or bridal arch of flowers. Elizabethan couples sat under a kissing knot, a wreath of herbs decorated with trailing ribbons, which was hung over them.

THE COMMITMENT

As I said in the introduction, the traditional handfasting is a trial marriage which may then be renewed with a more permanent commitment or abandoned. Modern Pagans often substitute the handfasting ceremony for a more conventional marriage ceremony, making the life long vows of marriage.

You need to consider the kind of vows that you will make to your beloved. Whether you will enter into the trial marriage of handfasting, or make a more permanent commitment.

The traditional handfasting promises include:
I give myself to (name) for a year and a day
> or
I give myself to (name) for thirteen moons
If you make this promise, you must see it through for one year. It is a solemn vow before the Gods. If you decide to go your separate ways after a year, you might simply part, or have a formal handparting.

You might not even want to make a time commitment at all, but say:
For as long as love shall last
> or
While we both shall love
This gives you the option to part before the year is up, stay together for a year, five years, twenty years, or the rest of your lives. If you decide to part, you might have a handparting ceremony if you both wish to.

If, after a year or more, you want to make a more permanent commitment, you might perform the handfasting again, saying either something like:
While love shall last
Or if you think you really have found your soul mate, you might make a lifetime declaration such as:
For this lifetime
> or
Until we are parted by death

Once again, remember that you are making a solemn vow before the Gods, and I would urge you to think very carefully indeed before undertaking it. Though people take vows and oaths lightly in today's society and think nothing of breaking them, this is not the way of the Pagan, whose oath is made before the Old Gods and is unbreakable, a matter of honour. If you make a solemn vow before the Gods and break it, there will be a heavy karmic price to pay, so think carefully before making any promise. A handparting is not the same as a divorce, and does not negate your oath. An oath that you make thinking that you can take it back later is not an oath, and the Gods see into your heart, even if no one else does.

Please do not even consider the entirely modern practice of soul binding, which binds the couple's souls together throughout all future incarnations as part of the rite. I believe this latter practice to be highly dangerous and very wrong. I have known people bound in this way to handpart after their year and a day, finding that their love was merely physical attraction and not the deep love of the *anam cara* of the 'soul friend' but, calamitously, because of their soul binding, they are doomed to go throughout life after life, meeting, mating and parting in disappointment. If you are truly twin souls, then you will meet time after time anyway, perhaps not in every incarnation, but as you are meant to for your individual developments.

Chapter 3
THE RITUALS

Handfastings are conducted in a circle, itself an important Pagan symbol. It has no beginning and no end. It is eternal. When the magician casts a circle, he or she creates a space apart from ordinary life: an interface between the mundane plane of waking consciousness and the realm of the gods and spirits, which we might call the Otherworld. When he or she enters the circle he leaves the ordinary world behind and enters a domain apart: a realm of sacred space and time. When the magic circle is properly built, cast and invoked, it becomes the universe in microcosm i.e. it creates in miniature the entire cosmos. The complete circle represents its oneness, while the divisions of the circle stand for the passing of time and the seasons, the space in which the universe exists, and the substances and energies of which it is made. Whatever the magician performs within this magical microcosm will be reflected in the macrocosm, or in other words, each ritual act will be made manifest in the macrocosm, whether it is the re-enactment of a seasonal myth or the love of two people which will echo throughout the Universe.

THE PERFECT CIRCLE
The circle is a universal symbol of wholeness and completion. The whole circle symbolises continuity, eternity, completion and spacelessness: the absence of time and space. As it symbolises what is complete and unbroken, it also symbolises the Deity and everlasting love. Mark the perimeter of the circle with flowers, crystals, pink, white or red candles, or shells. You can also scatter petals around the circle after it has been ritually swept.

But the circle can be divided: halved, quartered, or separated into degrees and so on. However, far from symbolising dissolution and imperfection, when these fractions are contained within the circle they represent the balance and harmony of such divisions. Think of the famous yin yang symbol, which represents the reconciliation of opposites within the whole. Within the circle,

16

opposites (such as day and night, summer and winter) are united. Within the circle their division is not absolute, but each gives rise to the other, reconciled in the circle of unity, just as the two halves of the couple make up the whole.

THE CARDINAL POINTS

The four main compass points of the circle are called the cardinal points. When the magic circle is drawn, it is aligned to the cardinal points of the compass—north, south, east and west. This is not merely symbolic, and the east of the circle should be aligned with the real east and so on. The flow of earth power is north to south. The North Star stands still at the north of the circle and for the Celts it was Caer Arianrhod, the Castle of the Silver Wheel, the entrance to the Otherworld and the place of death and rebirth. The circle must be orientated with the energies of the cosmos.

When the circle is cast by the magician, each direction is invoked in turn and the circle is thus spatially orientated. This operation is often called the summoning or invocation of the Watchtowers.

North

The north is the point of the circle associated with the winter solstice (Yule), cold, darkness, midnight, starlight, regeneration, rebirth and life through death, as it is at the winter solstice that the sun is reborn. It then gains strength and grows stronger up until the summer solstice. The north is associated with the element of earth. Place a dish of salt, soil, pebbles or a large stone or crystal in the north.

East

The east is the point of the circle associated with the spring equinox. The east is associated with sunrise, dawn and gestation, the beginning of growth; a time of green youth. It is connected with the element of air. In a stone circle oriented to the vernal equinox, the sun will rise directly in the east, over the east stone at the equinox. Place a dish of incense or a feather in the east.

South

The south is the point of the circle associated with the summer solstice, with the zenith of the sun's strength, midday, with things beginning to ripen, with maturity and the prime of life. It is connected with the element of fire. Place a lighted candle in the south.

West

The west is the point of the circle associated with the autumn equinox and the completion of the harvest, with twilight, sunset, and decline. It is associated with the element of water. Place a dish or cup of water in the west. You could float some rose petals on the surface of the water.

THE DIRECTIONS OF ABOVE AND BELOW

The celestial realms of above, and the underworld realm of below stand above and below the circle, and their powers are called upon, drawn through the cosmic axis of the circle as the first step of its casting. Thus the invoked circle is not a two dimensional object, but a sphere, extending below ground and above, in which the magician operates.

THE CENTRE OF THE CIRCLE

The central point represents the place where all powers meet, where all times and places are one. For the Celts it was the spiral or glass castle, a place of regeneration and rebirth. The axis through the centre links all the realms and times. The cardinal points are often called the quarters, which are further associated with the four elements. These are invoked when the circle is cast, so that the ring becomes a place of balanced energies.

The four Royal Roads of Power coming from the cardinal points meet at the centre of the circle. This point becomes the cosmic axis, the centre of all things where all times and places are one, from which all things are accessible. It may be symbolised by the pillar, the shaman's ladder, the world tree or cauldron of renewal.

THE ALTAR

Set up the altar in the northern quarter of the circle. A low table or chest can be employed. Cover it with a pink or red cloth and scatter it with rose petals. Place three pink candles (for love) in holders on the altar, or use red (for passion) or green (for the heart charka and unconditional love). A dish of salt and a dish of water are placed near the front. You will also need a knife which you keep for ritual purposes, which some people call an athame. You can also decorate the altar with flowers, greenery, fruit, nuts, heart shapes and so on. The chalice should be filled with red wine, or you can go the whole way, and fill it with champagne. Place the book of rituals where you can see it. You will also need the silken cords for binding, the rings and equipment for any other traditions you wish to include.

CREATING THE CIRCLE

(This is only one method of casting a circle, and there are many others, but the principle of establishing a boundary between the mundane world and a sacred space where ritual acts are carried out remains the same.)

A candle is placed in each of the quarters, the colours chosen help to resonate with the vibration of that quarter- green for the north (earth), yellow for the west (air), red for the south (fire) and blue for the west (water). If you can't get these you can use white candles, but the more you can re-enforce the imagery the more it helps your visualisation. Check that you have everything you need within the circle (remember the matches!) before you start, as once the circle is cast, you will not be able to leave to get it.

Sweep the circle with the broom. If you like, you can then scatter it with flower petals.

CASTING THE CIRCLE:

Light the incense. The first act that must be performed is to establish the boundaries of the circle. Take the knife and beginning in the north draw the circle round the room. Remember where the point of the knife draws will be the edge of the circle. Include in the circle all the things and people you wish to be within the circle.

I conjure the O circle of power that thou mayest be a meeting place of love and joy and truth a boundary between the world of men and the realms of the Otherworld, containing the power that we shall raise within thee, be a shield and protection against our enemies, both visible and invisible.

Take the knife and place the tip in the bowl of salt saying:

Be this salt dedicated to the Lord and Lady (or whatever deities you call upon) *to keep us from evil and protect us in this time.*

Take the knife again and place the tip in the bowl of water:

Be this water dedicated to the Lord and Lady (or whatever deities you call upon) *to keep us from peril and to purify this place.*

Tip the water into the salt and mix them together. Sprinkle clockwise (deosil) around the circle saying:

May we cast from us all evil and darkness, viciousness and malice. May we become that which we must be before the Lord and Lady (or whatever deities you call upon), *seeking ill to no one. May we be clean within and without so that we are acceptable before them.*

Finish by sprinkling each person in turn.

Next connect the circle to all three realms. Take the knife and stand in the centre of the circle. Point it above and say:

Powers of the worlds above, I do summon, stir and call you up to guard our circle and to witness our rites.

Bring the knife down in a straight line and point it downwards. Say:

Powers of the worlds below, I do summon, stir and call you up to guard our circle and to witness our rites.

The watchtowers are then invoked. Take the knife and begin in the north. The casting of the circle is always begun in the north as this is the place of power that flows from north to south, so the power gateway is opened. Many people do not begin the invocations until reaching the east, as this is the direction of vocalisation. Draw a pentacle in the east and say:

Oh mighty powers of the east, I do summon, stir and call you up to guard our circle and to witness our rites.

Repeat this in the south, west, and north.

Return to the altar and consecrate the altar candles with the words:
I consecrate these candles that they shall represent light and knowledge within this circle.

Light the candles and take one round to light all the quarter candles. If you wish you can carry the dish of incense around the circle.

The work of the ritual is now performed.

DISSOLVING THE CIRCLE
When all is finished the circle is dissolved. Take the knife and cut through the boundary of the circle near the east and say:

Mighty powers of the east, thank you for guarding our circle and for witnessing our rites. I bless you in the name of the Lord and the Lady (or whatever deities you call upon).

Repeat in all the other directions. Cut through the centre and thank the powers of above and below. Put out the candles and dismantle the temple.

HANDFASTING RITUALS

The rituals in this book are included to give you some basic outlines for the ceremony and a few ideas to start you off. Remember that this is your special day, and that you should tailor it to your needs. In particular, you should create your own vows, words that express your feelings, and which will be much more meaningful than anything I could write.

A PAGAN HANDFASTING

The circle is laid out as a ring of flowers by the bridesmaids. In the north, which represents the element of earth and the physical realm, they place a dish of salt and bread. In the east, which represents the element of air and the mental realm, they place a feather and the dish of incense, lighting it. In the south, which represents the element of fire and the realm of will, they place a candle. In the west, which represents the realm of water and the emotions, they place a cup of water. They wait inside the circle.

The presiding priest or priestess enters the circle followed by the bride and groom, the groomsman and other guests. The groom stands to the left of the bride, the best man slightly to one side and behind him, the bridesmaid to one side and slightly behind the bride. Non-Pagan guests may prefer to watch from outside the circle, but this is up to the couple, priest/ess and the guests themselves.

Priest/ess: *"We are gathered here to witness the handfasting of (name) and (name) in the presence of the Old Gods, and their brothers and sisters of the Old Ways. Be welcome all those who come in perfect love and perfect trust. We call upon our lovely Lady of the Silver Moon and our gentle Lord of the Wildwood to be present here today to bless this act of love celebrated in their honour. So shall it be."*

All: *"So shall it be".*

The priest/ess takes the couple and presents them to each of the quarters as follows:
"Spirits of the north, you spirits of earth. Know that (name) and (name) stand before you to seek the bond of handfasting. We ask you to witness this solemn rite. So shall it be."

All: *"So shall it be"*

The priest/ess takes the couple and presents them to the east:
"Spirits of the east, you spirits of air. Know that (name) and (name) stand before you to seek the bond of handfasting. We ask you to witness this solemn rite. So shall it be."

21

All: *"So shall it be"*

The priest/ess takes the couple and presents them to the south:
"Spirits of the south, you spirits of fire. Know that (name) and (name) stand before you to seek the bond of handfasting. We ask you to witness this solemn rite. So shall it be."

All: *"So shall it be"*

The priest/ess takes the couple and presents them to the west:
"Spirits of the west, you spirits of water. Know that (name) and (name) stand before you to seek the bond of handfasting. We ask you to witness this solemn rite. So shall it be."

All: *"So shall it be"*

They are then led to the altar where the rings (if used) are laid on the book of rituals. The priest/ess takes up the book and rings, and says:
"The ring is the perfect circle, whole and unbroken. I bless these rings in the name of the God and Goddess, that they symbolise the bond of true love between (name) and (name)."

Priest/ess: (to the man) *"(Name) is it your wish that you shall become handfast to (name) before the Old Gods?*

Groom: *"It is my wish to be handfast to (name) before the Old Gods and these witnesses."*

Priest/ess: *"And do you pledge on your honour, and before the Old Gods and these witnesses, that you will ever strive for her happiness, placing it above your own from this day forward, for as long as love shall last between you?"*

Groom: *"I do so swear on my honour before the Old Gods and these witnesses that I will ever strive for (name's) happiness, placing it above my own from this day forward, for as long as love shall last between us."*

Priest/ess: *"Then place your ring on her finger."* (The groom does so.)

Priest/ess: (to the woman) *"(Name) is it your wish that you shall become handfast to (name) before the Old Gods?*

Bride: *"It is my wish to be handfast to (name) before the Old Gods and these witnesses."*

Priest/ess: *"And do you pledge on your honour, and before the Old Gods and these witnesses, that you will ever strive for his happiness, placing it above your own from this day forward, for as long as love shall last between you?"*

Bride: *"I do so swear on my honour before the Old Gods and these witnesses that I will ever strive for (name's) happiness, placing it above my own from this day forward, for as long as love shall last between us."*

Priest/ess: *"Then place your ring on his finger."* (The bride does so.)

The priest/ess takes the cords and fastens the hands of the bride and groom together saying: *"You are bound together by the rite of handfasting in the eyes of the Old Gods and the Old Ways. Ever love and help one another as you have promised here today. May the God and Goddess bless you. Blessed Be."*

All: *"Blessed Be."*

The priest/ess takes the couple and presents them to each of the quarters as follows:
"Spirits of the north, you spirits of earth. Know that (name) and (name) share the bond of handfasting. Bestow on them, we beseech you, your gifts of plenty, good health and fertility so that they shall always be happy together. So shall it be."

All: *"So shall it be"*
The couple eat some of the bread dipped in the salt.

The priest/ess takes the couple and presents them to the east:
"Spirits of the east, you spirits of air. Know that (name) and (name) share the bond of handfasting. Bestow on them, we beseech you, your gifts of knowledge, good communication and inspiration so that they shall always be able to talk to each other, and find pleasure in each other's company. So shall it be."

All: *"So shall it be"*
The couple are purified with the incense and are given the feather.

The priest/ess takes the couple and presents them to the south:
"Spirits of the south, you spirits of fire. Know that (name) and (name) share the bond of handfasting. Bestow on them, we beseech you, your gifts of passion, vitality and creativity, so that their desire for each other shall not wane. So shall it be."

All: *"So shall it be"*

The couple light the candle, holding the taper together.

The priest/ess takes the couple and presents them to the west:
"Spirits of the west, you spirits of water. Know that (name) and (name) share the bond of handfasting Bestow on them, we beseech you, your gifts of friendship, support and love. So shall it be."

All: *"So shall it be"*
The couple both drink from the cup and are led back to the altar.

Priest/ess:. *Let all of us now offer blessings and congratulations to (name) and (name)."*

Everyone speaks any prepared or spontaneous blessings they have and showers the couple with flower petals. The broom is brought forward and the couple encouraged to jump over it for luck.

Priest/ess: *"As it has been since the beginning of time, and as it shall be till the end, two lovers have been joined together, and by this have been made stronger, happier and greater than they were apart, and the simple fact that their love exists in the world benefits us all. This wondrous state is the gift of our gracious Lady and her own gentle Lord, whose love flows through all things, and whose passion we see reflected throughout the seasons, and which is the deepest mystery of our faith. "*

The bridesmaids open the flower circle.

Priest/ess: *"The circle is open but unbroken. What we have witnessed here today will remain in our hearts. We thank the spirits of north, south, east and west for their presence. We thank our gracious Lord and Lady for their blessings. Blessings be on all. So shall it be."*

All: *"So shall it be!"*

This is the signal for the feast and games to begin.

A WICCAN HANDFASTING
Place three pink candles in holders on the altar. A dish of salt and a dish of water are placed near the front. A plate of bread or cakes and some wine in an open bottle or jug are placed to one side. You will need a cup or goblet for drinking the wine and a pentacle of clay or copper. You will also need an athame.

A glass or clay cup is placed on the altar from which the couple will drink, then break as a token that no other shall share what they have together.

In addition the two rings are placed on the book of rituals. Flowers such as meadowsweet, apple blossom, violets, cherry blossom and roses are placed on the altar, about the circle and wreathed into chaplets for the couple and their guests.

Cast the circle in the usual manner.

The God and the Goddess are then invoked:

(Goddess name) I invoke and call upon thee, three fold Goddess of the moon, (Goddess name), Queen of the moonlit sea, fairer than night and silver clad, thee I invoke, Mother of the moon and calm waters, let thy light fall upon us for thy hair is a pool of stars in the darkness. I call upon thee, widow of the waning moon whose children have left thee to sorrow, guard us with learning and grant us a place in thy dark cloak of understanding. Thee I invoke. Descend I beseech thee and be with us now.

The God is then invoked:

(God name) Lord of the heaven and power of the sun. Lord of the hunt and forests. I invoke thee in thy secret name of (God name). Come unto us and honour our circle we beg of you. Mighty one, our Lord, all honour to thee, consort of the Goddess. Come, I call upon thee. Descend I beseech thee and be with us now.

The purpose of the ritual is then stated:

Lord and Lady, God and Goddess, sacred pair that were with us before the dawn of time and shall be till its dusk, hear now the purpose of this ritual and witness it. Two of your secret children wish to share the bond of handfasting, declaring their love before thee and their brothers and sisters of the Craft.

The circle dance is performed to raise power:

Thrice about the altar go
Once for Virgin pure as snow,
Once for Full Moon's soft sweet breath,
Once for Dark Moon, old as death,
Thrice about the altar spin
That the right shall well begin.

Priest: *Who among you seeks the bond of handfasting?*

25

Priestess: *Let them be named and brought forward.*

Groomsman: *(Name) is the man.*

Bridesmaid: *(Name) is the woman.*

Priestess: *(to groom) Are you (name)?*

Groom: *I am.*

Priestess: *And what is your desire?*

Groom: *To be handfast to (name) before the Lord and Lady, and my brothers and sisters of the Craft.*

Priest: *(to bride) Are you (name)?*

Bride: *I am.*

Priest: *And what is your desire?*

Bride: *To be handfast to (name) before the Lord and Lady, and my brothers and sisters of the Craft.*

Priestess: (holds the coven sword or her athame aloft) *Aradia, Cernunnos* [4] *here before you stand two of your secret people. Witness now what they have to declare* (she places the sword or athame at the groom's chest) *repeat after me: I (name) do come here of my own free will to seek the partnership of (name). I come with all honour, love and sincerity, wishing only to become one with her whom I love. Always will I strive for (name's) happiness and welfare. Her life will I defend before my own. May this sword be plunged into my chest should I not be sincere in all that I declare. All this I swear before Cernunnos and Aradia. May they give me strength to keep my vows. So mote it be.*

The priest repeats the procedure with the bride.

The couple are anointed with handfasting oil.

If rings are used they are blessed by the priest and priestess at this point, in the name of the God and Goddess, and exchanged by the bride and groom who now make their own vows.

---

4   or whatever deity names your coven uses

A small cup of wine is brought forward:

Priestess: *Drink your fill of the cup of love.*

The cup is shared by the couple, which is then broken to denote than no other shall partake of what they have together. (Wrap the cup in a cloth to avoid dangerous flying shards, and have a small hammer ready to do the deed.)

The priest then binds their hands together with the cords saying: *Know that you are bound for a year and a day in the eyes of the Gods and your brothers and sisters of the Craft. You shall return in thirteen moons to this place to renew your vows or go your separate ways. Know that this is a solemn vow, and you are one. Love, honour and respect each other.*

Cakes and wine are blessed and shared by everyone present. The priestess takes the wine and pours it into the chalice: *Lord and Lady, I call upon you to bless this wine, the blood of the earth pressed smooth. As we drink of thee may we learn of the wisdom of the Goddess.*

The wine is passed round clockwise. She blesses the cakes:

Lord and Lady, I call upon thee the bless these cakes, the fruit of the womb of the Goddess without which we would not live. A we eat of thee may we learn of the love of the Goddess.

The cakes are passed round.

When all is finished the circle is dissolved. The priestess takes the knife and cuts through the boundary of the circle near the east and says: *Mighty powers of the east, thank you for guarding our circle and for witnessing our rites. I bless you in the name of the Lord and the Lady.*

This is repeated in all the other directions. She cuts through the centre and thank the powers of above and below. The Lord and Lady are not dismissed but thanked: *Companions, we have met together this night to celebrate the handfasting of (name) our brother and (name) our sister. Together we have worked for our purposes. The God and Goddess have witnessed our workings and only they will measure our purposes and our hearts. Together we have invoked for power to accomplish our working, but it is not for us to command those whom we worship. Nor is it for us to bid them be gone. We cannot dismiss them. I ask instead of the Lord and Lady that they are with us all our days, guiding our feet and lighting our paths. I ask that the Lord and Lady are with us in our lives and in our deaths, our true parents, even as we are their children. Let the circle be extinguished but let us not forget the workings of this night. Let the candles be put out but let us not forget what we have learned. Let the rite be ended now in the knowledge we shall meet once more.*

Before the Lord and Lady (God and Goddess name), God and Goddess, the rite is ended. Blessed Be.

The broomstick is brought forward and the couple are jokingly told that they must jump over once for each child they wish to have. They are showered with rice, rose petals, meadowsweet, violets, wheat and orange blossom, etc.

ALTERNATIVE HANDFASTING RITUAL

Lay out a circle of crystals (ideally rose quartz). Cast the circle in the usual manner.

Priest: *We call upon the Lord whom we worship, Angus Og, the young god of love who sparks desire. Be with us to witness the joining of (name) and (name) in the rite of handfasting.*

Priestess: *We call upon our Lady, the beautiful Aine, the goddess of love, white fingered and sensual. Be with us to witness the joining of (name) and (name) in the rite of handfasting.*

Priest: (to bride) *Do you come here freely to seek the bond of handfasting with (name)?*

Bride: *I do.*

Priestess: (to groom) *Do you come here freely to seek the bond of handfasting with (name)?*

Groom: *I do.*

Priest: *Then before the Gods and these witnesses, I bind you with this cord. It is the bond of love alone which joins you. Let it not be a restriction but a loving sharing. Stand together, but not too close, for nothing thrives in the shadow of another. Listen to the music of the other's heart and appreciate it for its own beauty, and do not insist that your songs are the same. Let your love stand firm, like the mountains of the earth; let it sing like the wind in the trees and burn like the midsummer fires. Let your love flow like the tides of the sea, freely and always moving, soul to soul.*

The couple face each other and declare:
*I offer you my body, that we may know pleasure together
I share with you my mind, that we may find wisdom together
I open my soul to you, that we may grow in spirit together*

28

I offer you my heart, that we may love, wholly and unselfishly, each other.
So mote it be.

All: *So mote it be.*

The couple may exchange rings, gifts and so on if desired. The cakes and wine follow. The God and Goddess are thanked:

Priestess: *We thank you, Aine, for your presence here tonight. Give each of us your gift of love; let each of us find the one who makes us more than we are, who brings us joy and happiness.*

Priest: *We thank you Angus Og, for your presence here tonight. Give us your gift of love, let each of us find it within our hearts to love, to be the lover, to be loved.*

The circle is broken and the party begins.

LEGAL HANDFASTING IN THE UK

A handfasting ceremony can constitute a legal marriage in the UK providing certain conditions are met:

- The ceremony needs to take place in a venue registered for marriages. These include many hotels, castles and spiritual venues, such as the Beacon in Nuneaton, Warks which conducts legal handfastings (see the Resources Section at the end of the book).
- A Registrar must be present. The registrar must be booked in advance and a fee paid.
- It is a legal requirement to give notice in advance of marriage or civil partnership. Your notice is publicly displayed for fifteen days, after which the authority for your marriage or civil partnership can be granted. Each notice is valid for one year, but if you decide to change venue, new notices must be given. If you are having a civil marriage or civil partnership, you both need to go to your local register office to give notice. If you plan holding your marriage or civil partnership in a different area, you should also contact the local register office for that area before you give notice, to ensure that officials will be available on the day. You both must give notice in person - no one else can do it on your behalf. If you are giving notice in Wales, you may give this in English, or in English and Welsh. If notice is to be given bilingually, both the couple giving notice and the officer must be able to understand the Welsh language. All local authorities in Wales have at least one

Welsh speaking officer or deputy. Before you give notice, you should make sure that you are able to satisfy the laws concerning residency and immigration control.[5]

- Each of the parties must make a declaration in one of the following forms:
  (a) By Saying "I do solemnly declare that I know not of any lawful impediment why I (name) may not be joined in matrimony to (name)." OR
  (b) By saying "I declare that I know of no legal reason why I (name) may not be joined in marriage to (name) OR
  (c) By saying "I am." To the question put to them successively "Are you (name) free lawfully to marry (name)?"
- That each of them says to the other one of the following form of words of contract:
  (a) "I call upon these persons here present, to witness that I (name) take you to be my lawful wedded wife (or husband)." OR
  (b) I (name) take you (or thee) (name) to be my lawful wedded wife (or husband)."

THE GREAT RITE

The Great Rite is a ritualised use of the sexual act (in actuality or more usually in a purely symbolic form) for magical purposes. It is the supreme joining of the male and female energies that shape the cosmos, the flowing and joining of those energies. Between two people it is a deep connection whereby they open to each other physically and spiritually. Sexual union between two people can be a transcendent experience in which they touch the divine within.[6] For the Pagan sex is not shameful or considered a taboo subject, but is a joyful celebration of being part human and part divine. The body is not something to be despised, but a great gift to celebrated.

Some witches from the newer traditions seem to think that the Great Rite is only used during initiation ceremonies, especially the third degree rite. This is not true. Starhawk called sex a Wiccan sacrament, the "*deep connection and recognition of the wholeness of another person…an exchange of energy, of subtle nourishment, between people*".[7] It may be used to raise energy for magic, conceive a magical child or to consummate a handfasting. If it is to be symbolic, this takes the form of the athame (the witch's ritual knife), a masculine emblem, plunged into a

5   http://www.direct.gov.uk/en/Governmentcitizensandrights/Registeringlifeevents/Marriagesandcivilpartnerships
6   Lira Silbury, *The Sacred Marriage*, Llewellyn, St Paul, 1994
7   Starhawk, *The Spiral Dance*

chalice which is a feminine image of the womb of the Goddess. This may be part of the handfasting ritual witnessed by the coven. If the Great Rite is to take place in actuality, this will be when everyone else has gone home, and the bride and groom are in the privacy of their chamber. The bedroom too can be a sacred temple.

RENEWING THE VOWS

If the handfasting vow is for a year and a day, then the vows should be renewed after that time elapses. Another full ceremony can be held, with coven and witnesses present or it may be a simple exchange of vows between the two people concerned. This time the couple may wish to make a more permanent arrangement or merely renew the arrangement for another year and a day. Otherwise, the handfasting lapses after thirteen moons and the couple is free to go their separate ways with no recriminations. If both people agree, then a handparting ritual may be held to bring closure to the relationship.

Chapter 4
GODS AND GODDESSES

Wiccans and most Pagans worship the Goddess and the God equally. The Goddess is the creator of the Universe, giving birth to it from her cosmic womb, and annually gives birth to the God, who grows to manhood, marries the goddess and dies in the autumn, to be buried in the tomb which is her womb, and which brings him once again to rebirth in the Eternal Return of the seasons. He is the sun and the corn, the lord of the wildwood. This is the oldest story in the world.

Together the Goddess and the God represent the whole of creation. He is male, she is female, he is the sun, she is the moon, he is the sky and she is the earth nourished by his fertilising rain. Pagans believe in a kind of cosmic harmony of opposing forces held in dynamic equilibrium, the male energy of the God and the female energy of the Goddess. The relationship of the God and Goddess is reflected in the loves of human couples. Together the two opposites make one perfect whole, the two together capable of far more than each alone. Each person must recognise the divine part of themselves that is the Goddess or the God, and their partners must recognise it in each other. Only in this way can a sacred partnership be formed 'in perfect love and perfect trust' as we are instructed that we must come before the Gods. The God and Goddess are honoured within the other.

THE BRIDE AND THE GODDESS

During the sacred rite of handfasting, the bride represents the Goddess and for that moment, she is the Goddess in her bridal aspect, her love uplifting and changing everyone present, but especially her bridegroom. The man recognises the Goddess in his bride and approaches her with love and great respect. She is not his chattel as in a Christian ceremony and she does not promise to obey him. They are equal partners in life. Together they are the balance of male and female, day and night, summer and winter, sun and moon, sky and earth, the comic harmony which they are re-enacting, two perfect halves of one whole. Like the

Goddess, the bride may create life if she chooses, or may fashion works of art, objects, crafts or books. Moreover, she brings the radiant love of the Goddess into a home. Like the Goddess she is powerful, loving and strong, intuitive, a healer, a teacher. Like the moon, her womb waxes and wanes each month. She is the maiden of the waxing moon, innocent, independent and carefree. She is the vital mother of the full moon, voluptuous, sensuous, passionate and fruitful. She is the mysterious powerful crone, wise and all knowing, the incomparable seer who can pierce the veils between the worlds.

The bride should take some time to connect to this part of herself before the wedding, working for several weeks with this loving expansive energies of the Goddess that dwells within her, and which she manifests.

THE GROOM AND THE GOD

The groom represents the God during the ritual. The bride sees the God in her husband and in every man. He is strong and powerful, gentle and loving. He is not afraid of the emotions within, and can express love and tears, happiness and sadness in equal measure. He is the poet, the dancer and the shaman. He is the fire of the sun, the lord of the hunt, the stag of seven tines, the protector and the protected, the son, the lover and the husband. He is the wildfire, the untamed spirit of the forest in his heart.

The groom should spend a few weeks before the ceremony connecting with the God, and the God within.

GODDESSES OF LOVE

The bride might like to work on building a special bond with one of the goddesses of love in the weeks and months prior to the handfasting. During the ceremony, you can agree with the celebrant to invoke one of these deities:

ABUNDIA is an Italian witch goddess, or some say Queen of the Fairies. She appears as a lovely woman with dark hair wearing a circlet with a star on her forehead. She is a fertility goddess who bestows abundance on earth.

AINE is an Irish goddess of love and fertility who took many mortal lovers. Her name means 'brightness', 'heat', or 'speed', indicating that she is a sun goddess and the word *Ain* is cognate with the Latin *ignis*, meaning 'fire'. Her festival is Midsummer, marked by a torchlight procession about her hill led by young women and a bonfire vigil. When she was pursued by St Patrick's hounds she scattered her perfume on meadowsweet to confuse them, and so gave the flower its scent. It is one of the herbs of love.

AKKA (Finish) is the wife of the supreme god Ukko. Akka is the goddess of the harvest, agriculture, love, women and female sexuality. She is an Earth Mother.

APHRODITE is the Greek goddess of love and desire. She is supremely beautiful and no man or woman can resist her charms. Her magic is the rapture of love and sexual ecstasy. She was 'foam-born' (*aphros*) from the sea, rising naked and accompanied by doves and sparrows. She sailed to shore on a scallop shell, emerging from the sea near Paphos on the island of Cyprus. It is likely that she was originally an eastern fertility goddess adopted into the Olympian pantheon.

Her attributes are the dolphin, the dove, the swan, the pomegranate, sparrow, goose, partridge, wryneck, swan, rose, myrtle, quince, rose campion, water mint, plane, cypress and bay. Her metal is copper.

The fact that she renews her virginity in a spring after each sexual encounter proclaims her to be an earth mother/fertility goddess, who gives birth each year to the crops, and is renewed in the springtime, washed clean by the spring rains. Her domain seems to have encompassed the fertility of animals, plants and human beings. As the world grew more patriarchal and prudish, Aphrodite's gifts and orgiastic nature was looked upon with contempt or horror, but originally her rites were sacred. Sex constituted a sacred act, and was the proper way to honour the goddess of love and desire. The patriarchal Greeks stripped away all her other attributes, leaving her the goddess of love, ostensibly of married love as Aphrodite Benetrix, encompassing spiritual or ideal love as Aphrodite Urania ('Heavenly Aphrodite'), but also as the goddess of lust and the patroness of prostitutes as Aphrodite Porne. Her chief festival was called the 'Aphrodisiac', a word that is still familiar to us today.

Her attributes are the dolphin, the dove, the swan, the pomegranate, sparrow, goose, partridge, wryneck, swan, rose, myrtle, quince, rose campion, water mint, plane, cypress and bay. Her metal is copper.

ASHTART is the Canaanite goddess of sexuality, fertility, love, war and the hunt. She is the consort of Baal, and also a goddess of war and the chase. In Sidon she merited royal priests and   priestesses.

ATHYR (Hindu) gave birth to the universe. She is a goddess of love and beauty.

BAST is the ancient Egyptian cat-headed goddess of pleasure, fire, childbirth, fertility, joy, sex, fertility, music, dance, protection, laughter, healing, intuition, marriage and animals. She is one of the oldest Egyptian goddesses, known as the daughter and 'Eye of Ra'. Herodotus, writing in the mid 5th century BCE, described the festival at Bubastis in the eastern Delta. He said that 700,000 people (not including children) attended it. People sang and played music, drank wine and made sacrifices, paying their respects to the goddess in her red granite temple. Dead cats were taken there to be embalmed and buried in order to carry messages from their

34

owners to the gods. She was shown dressed in green holding a sistrum (a rattle) in her right hand and a basket in her left, often with kittens at her feet.

BRANWEN ("White Raven") is the Welsh goddess of love, the sister of the alder god Bran ("Raven") who was the guardian of all Britain. In the *Mabinogion* stories she was called a 'fair maiden' one of the most beautiful women in the world, and one of the three chief ladies (sovereign goddesses) of the land.

DEMETER ('Earth Mother') is the Greek goddess of agriculture, fertility and marriage. Her priestesses initiated the bride and groom into the secrets of the marriage bed. Demeter rules the cycle of the year, the phases of the moon, the seasons and the life of man, ordering them all in their time. This makes her a goddess of stability, law and order, a state which extends into fidelity and marriage. The women of Greece celebrated the feast of Thesmophoria (*thesmophoros*, "she of the regular customs") in her honour. In ancient art, Demeter was often portrayed as a solemn woman, wearing a wreath of braided ears of wheat.

DIONE (Greek) is the daughter of Uranus and Gaia and the mother of Aphrodite. She is the goddess of prophecy and love.

FREYA ("Lady" /" Mistress") is the Scandinavian goddess who gave her name to the sixth day of the week, Friday. She is usually depicted in a flowing gown and sometimes a feathered cloak and shining jewelled necklace. She is the goddess of love, and lends a favourable ear to the prayers of lovers. Love songs were always composed in her honour, and in Germany, her name became the verb which meant 'to woo'. She is a goddess of lust; Loki accused her of sleeping with all the gods in turn. She even mated with Loki in the form of a flea. She enjoys sexual freedom, taking her choice of lovers among gods and mortals at will.

She is married to the god Odur, who is a marvellous lover, and represents passion and the pleasures of sexual love. He also symbolises the summer sun. When he is with her, she is happy and content, but he once disappeared and she was forced to hunt for him in a story reminiscent of the search of Demeter for Persephone, and Ishtar for Tammuz. Freya wept tears of gold and amber as she wandered around the world seeking news of his whereabouts. Without the god and goddess, icy winter gripped the earth. Eventually she found Odur beneath a myrtle tree in the southern lands. They were reunited and Freya became as happy as a bride, which is why brides in the northern lands wear myrtle in preference to orange blossom. As they journeyed home, the grass grew green again, the flowers blossomed and nature rejoiced.

FRIGG (Norse) is the wife of the chief god Odin. She is a goddess of marriage, fertility, sexuality, love and motherhood.

GAIA (Greek), whose name means "Deep Breasted" because of her nurturing qualities, is the Earth itself. She created the universe, the first race of gods and humans. She represents love and fertility, and presides over marriages.

HATHOR ("House of Horus") is the ancient Egyptian goddess of joy, motherhood, love, beauty (copper mirrors had an image of her on their handles), dance, music and the arts in general. She protected pregnant women. Hathor and Horus are husband and wife. Their Sacred Marriage was celebrated on the eighteenth day of Paoni, the tenth month. The image of Hathor was taken from her Temple at Dendera and sailed to the temple of Horus at Edfu. Then Horus would leave his temple and greet Hathor on the river. The main event was the consummation of the marriage. Hathor's earliest form was probably the cow. Sometimes she is shown as entirely animal, at others as a cow headed woman, or with just a pair of cow horns encircling the solar disc, or just cow's ears as she was shown at Dendera and Philae.

HERA ("Lady"/ "Protectress") is the Greek goddess of marriage. Zeus found and courted her at Knossos in Crete. She took pity on him when he appeared as a bedraggled cuckoo, and she warmed him in her breast. He immediately assumed his true shape and made love to her, and so afterwards they were married. The gods all brought wedding gifts, and the wedding night was spent on Samos and lasted three hundred mortal years. She bathes in the spring at Canathus, near Argos, to renew her virginity. She carried a pomegranate in her left hand to symbolise the death of the year, and a cuckoo topped sceptre in her right hand to symbolise the regeneration of the year in spring. Her renewal bath has similar connotations.

ISHTAR is the Mesopotamian goddess of life and death. She rules sexual activity, ovulation and the menstrual cycle. She is depicted sitting on a lapis lazuli throne wearing a necklace with a star, accompanied by doves. Sometimes she is shown riding on a lion, her sacred animal. As the goddess of love, her symbol was the eight-pointed star (the planet Venus) or a rosette. The zodiac was known as the "girdle of Ishtar".

    The most famous story of Ishtar tells of her search for Tammuz in the Underworld, a legend recorded on clay tablets around 1750 BCE, which recalls the search of Demeter for Persephone. He was her husband and died every year during the hot month of Tammuz (July-August), gored by a boar. His soul was taken to the underworld and the goddess Ishtar led the lamentation, but the whole world mourned his death. The earth became dry and barren, as all vegetation withered in the blistering heat. Ishtar decided that she must go into the underworld to rescue her husband from the clutches of Ereshkigal, but despite the fact she relinquished her clothes and jewels, she was also taken prisoner. Meanwhile the earth was arid, barren and joyless. Sin the moon god and Shamash the sun god decided that something had to be done. They asked Ea, the god of water, magic and wisdom to help; he sent a messenger into the underworld with a powerful spell. The goddess of the underworld was forced to release her captives. Ishtar was purified by Ea's waters and passed back through the seven gates, regaining her raiment and jewels at each. Joy returned to earth [8] and life began anew as the first rains fell around the autumn equinox, when the festival of the "Holy Marriage" was celebrated.

ISIS ("Throne") is the Egyptian goddess of marriage, motherhood, healing, magic, prophecy, love, fertility, agriculture, domestic crafts, spinning, weaving and brewing. Like other magical goddesses, Isis is associated with spinning and weaving, drawing out concepts into being, and weaving or knotting various forces to control them. Isis taught humanity the art of using magical knots. It has been said that the priestesses of Isis could control the weather simply by braiding and releasing their hair. One of her symbols is the *tiet*, which is also called the "Isis-knot" and "the Blood of Isis" and is associated with her menstrual blood or womb and vagina. In shape it looks like an ankh with the arms folded down. It is sometimes considered the knot of fate.

Isis and Osiris ruled on earth, teaching humankind how to plant and harvest grain, how to spin and weave, make tools, bread, beer and wine. They also established the institution of marriage, religious ritual, and rescued the inhabitants of Egypt from the barbarous customs of cannibalism. All this time, the kingdom was peaceful and prosperous, but trouble was brewing. Their brother Set grew jealous and hatched a plot with seventy two co-conspirators. They invited Osiris to a party. When the festivities were in full swing, Set caused a beautiful coffin to be brought into the room, declaring that whoever could perfectly fit into the coffin should own it. Everyone tried it, since it was a magnificent piece of workmanship, but it fitted no one. Then everyone called for the king to try it. Osiris duly stepped into it and lay down. Instantly, the lid was slammed shut and nailed down. Osiris suffocated within and died, going into the afterlife and becoming the ruler of the dead. Set's followers took the coffin and threw it in the Nile, hoping it would sink. Instead it sailed away. After

---

8 Witches will recognize this story as the descent of the Goddess into the Underworld.

many adventures, Isis found the coffin and set about reviving Osiris, beating her wings to force air into his lifeless lungs, and trying to warm him with her own body, impregnating herself on the erect penis of Osiris, and conceiving the child Horus.

JUNO is the Roman Queen of Heaven, consort of the God Jupiter, invoked as *Optima Maxima*, i.e. 'best and greatest goddess'. She is the goddess of women, particularly married women, and oversees all aspects of a woman's life, from birth, youth, marriage and child-bearing to death. As the patroness of marriage, Juno restores peace between quarrelling couples. Her husband had many affairs, and this was her greatest grief; she insists that fidelity is part of marriage. One of her temples was a refuge for women treated badly by their husbands. She is a mother goddess, possibly of the full moon, and rules childbirth, blessing and guarding every child that is born, according to the Romans. Her own children are Mars, Hebe and Vulcan. Every year on the first of March, the married women of Rome held a festival called the *Matronalia* to honour the goddess and thank her for her blessings. They prayed for happy marriages and healthy babies.

LADA (Slavonic) the goddess of spring and love worshipped throughout Lithuania, Poland and Russia, the wife of the chief god of time and fate.

MAIA (Greek) is one of the seven daughters of Atlas and Hermes. She is the Goddess of the spring, youth and love. She was the eldest and loveliest of the famous Pleiades, or Seven Sisters. Zeus fell in love with her and fathered a son, Hermes.

OLWEN (Welsh) is the goddess of love and spring. She was the daughter of the giant Hawthorn who would tolerate no suitor for his daughter as he knew that if she should marry his life would come to an end. Kulwch, the son of a king, had no need to see her to fall in love with her, he blushed at her very name, and asked her father how he could obtain her in marriage. Eventually, after some fierce resistance, Hawthorn agreed to discuss the bride price of his daughter - thirteen treasures must be presented to him as a dowry. Though this was a terrible and dangerous task Kulwch agreed, and after many adventures the treasures were laid before the incredulous Hawthorn. The marriage of his daughter was of course the herald of his death. However, seeing all the quests completed he turned to Kulwch and said "*My daughter is yours. By my free will you should never have her, for with her I lose my life*". Thereupon he suffered his head to be cut off and it was put on a pole. The same night Olwen was Kulwch's bride.

OSHUN meaning 'Sweet Water' is the Nigerian goddess of rivers, a deity of fertility, love, beauty and sensual pleasures, the patroness of artists, witches and diviners. Hers are all the feminine powers and her symbols are the sacred drum which represents her womb, the crescent moon, the colour yellow, mirrors and cowrie shells. She is usually depicted as a tall coffee coloured woman, with seven bracelets, a mirror at her belt, carrying a pot of river water, and accompanied by a peacock. The Yoruba recognised that the cosmos is a perfect construct, and contains within it all possibilities. The types of energy within it number four hundred and one, with two hundred positive energies, two hundred negative energies, and one neutral energy that can express itself as either positive or negative. These are called Orisa and each one is a pure energy that may be expressed in human life in myriad ways. Oshun is the Orisa of pure joy, expressed in creativity, sensuality, beauty, childbirth and wealth.

QADESH ("Holy") is a Hittite goddess whose worship was introduced into Egypt in the New Kingdom. She is a moon goddess of love, sexual pleasure and ecstasy. She was depicted as a naked woman standing on the back of a lion holding flowers (or mirror) and snakes in her hands.

SJOFNA (Norse) Goddess of love and sex, also known as Vjofn. It was her duty to end quarrels between married couples.

VAR (Norse) Goddess of contracts and agreements who punishes those who break their oaths. She also symbolizes love.

XOCHIQUETZAL (Aztec) whose name means 'precious flower' was attractive and desirable, and her gifts were sexual pleasure, flowers and fertility. Brides braided their hair into a likeness of the two quetzal plumes that were sacred to her.

GODS OF LOVE

ADONIS (Greek) - God of vegetation, fertility, rebirth and the consort of Aphrodite. The cult of this vegetation god is generally thought to have originated in Syria, and his name is a variation on the Semitic *Adonai*, simply meaning 'Lord'. According to the most complete version of his story, the mortal King Cinyras boasted that his daughter Myrrha ('Myrrh') was more beautiful than Aphrodite, the goddess of love. As a punishment, the gods caused the unfortunate Myyrha to fall in love with her father. By a trick, she inveigled him into sleeping with her and getting her pregnant. When the king discovered what had happened he was overcome with disgust and guilt, and took up his sword to kill her. She fled from the palace, but he caught up with her on the brow of a hill. Just as he lifted the blade to strike her, the goddess Aphrodite took pity on the girl and instantly changed her into a myrrh tree, which the sword cleaved in two. [9] Out tumbled the infant Adonis. Aphrodite caught him up and concealed the lovely boy inside a chest, which she asked Persephone, the Queen of the Underworld, to look after. Overwhelmed with curiosity Persephone peeped inside the chest and instantly fell in love with the handsome youth she found there. When Aphrodite demanded that she return Adonis to her, Persephone refused, wanting to keep him for herself. Eventually the two goddesses appealed to Zeus (the king of the gods) to settle the quarrel. He appointed the muse Calliope to make the ruling and she decided that Aphrodite should have Adonis for one third of the year, Persephone for another third, and that he should have one third to himself. However, Aphrodite was not happy with this and decided to cheat. She donned her magic girdle, which caused all that looked upon her beauty to fall hopelessly in love with her; as a result, Adonis wanted to be with her all the time. Persephone reported this to Aphrodite's usual lover, the war god Ares, who flared up in a jealous rage. He transformed himself into a wild boar and tore Adonis to pieces.[10] From each drop of blood that fell, a red flower bloomed. [11] Zeus resolved to put an end to the squabbling and mayhem, and decreed that Adonis must spend the winter with Persephone, but could spend the summer with Aphrodite. When Adonis was with his beloved Aphrodite the land bloomed and the people rejoiced, but when he was with Persephone in the Underworld winter came and the people mourned. As in other fertility religions, it was the mating of the young god and goddess that made the earth blossom and fruit.

AENGUS MAC OG (Irish) the young god of love, son of the good god the Dagda, and Boann, goddess of the river Boyne and one of the Tuatha de Danaan. He lived in the tumulus of Newgrange in County Meath. His name means something like "vigorous son of youth". Some texts refer to him as one of the three sons of the Dagda. In the story of the Vision of Aengus (*Aislinge Oenguso*) he saw a lovely maiden in his dreams; before he could touch her she disappeared. These dreams went on for a year, and he became sick with love of her. His mother searched the length and breadth of Ireland in an attempt to find

---

9   Myrrh was a well know aphrodisiac and the birth of Adonis from myrrh indicates the orgiastic nature of his rites. The drops of gum shed by the myrrh represent the tears shed for him during the Adonia.

10   Though in some versions of the tale it is Artemis, the goddess of hunt and moon, who causes his death.

11   Identified as anemones or red roses.

the girl, but without success. Eventually, she summoned the Dagda to help, and the girl was located at the Galtee Mountains in Co. Tipperary. Her name was Caer Iobharmheith. It was explained to them that she was a swan maiden, who lived in the form of a bird on alternate years. They found her at Lough Beal Dragan at Samhain, accompanied by a hundred and fifty maidens linked by a silver chain. Her chain was of gold. Aengus became a swan himself, and they embraced and flew three times round the lake putting everyone in the vicinity asleep with their songs. He was the protector of the hero Diarmaid and rescued the eloping Diarmaid and Grainne from Fionn's men. Aengus forged four kisses into four birds which charmed the young people of Ireland.

AGNI (Hindu) the god of fire, purity and fertility who is part of the essence of all things, associated with sex and male virility. He loves all his worshippers equally, visiting their hearths.

ANTEROS (Roman) the God of mutual love who punishes those who do not return love.

CERUNNOS (Gaulish) a god of fertility, animals, wild places, love, birth, death and rebirth. He is depicted as a stag headed man holding a torc in one hand and a and snake in the other.

CUPID (Roman) the god of physical love, the son of Venus, usually equated with the Greek Eros. His name comes from *cupido* meaning 'desire' and he was also known as *Amor* or "love". He wore a blindfold to suggest that the arrows of love he shot into human beings hit at random in a way often considered as mischievous. Ovid wrote in *Amores* and the *Art of Love*:

"Cupid's there, quiver reversed, bow broken,
Holding a burnt-out torch.
See how sadly he walks, poor child, wings drooping,
How he beats at his bared breast,
How the tears rain down on his hair, now lying all tangled
About his throat, and his mouth's a loud O of grief.
Thus he looked, they say, long ago, when he saw his
Brother Aeneas to the grave..."

EROS (Greek) was considered to be the son of Aphrodite, and is the god of sex and desire, his name giving us the word 'erotic'. He has a golden bow and arrows, which he fires at humans and gods alike, making them fall in love. According to the Greek poet Hesiod,

"...Eros, the fairest of the deathless gods;
he unstrings the limbs and subdues both mind
and sensible thought in the breasts of all gods and all men." [12]

Eros was one of the first deities born into the world. The *Theogony* claims
that Eros emerged from Chaos along with Gaia (the Earth) and Tartarus (the
Underworld) and this makes it clear that neither god nor man may resist the
power of Eros, making him one of the most powerful of the gods.

FAUNUS (Roman) is a Roman nature spirit and patron of the fields and
shepherds. He prophesies through the whispering of the wind in the trees. He
is the leader of the *Fauni*, and may be compared with the Greek Pan. Like many
nature spirits he is half man, half goat in appearance. His female counterpart is
called Fauna or Faula.

FU-HSING (Chinese) The god of love, success and good fortune. He is also
called Fuk the Star God of Happiness and Wealth. His sacred animal is the bat.

KAMA (Hindu) the god of love who sprang directly from the heart of Brahma
the creator, or some say he is the son of Lakshmi. He is the god of love, lust
and desire and is married to Rati, the goddess of sexual desire, and to Priti, the
goddess of pleasure. He has a bow made of sugar cane strung with honey bees,
and five flower tipped arrows that inflame the five senses and inspire love in
anyone they hit. His chief festival is the *Madonatsava* and he is invoked by brides
when they leave the parental home. He gives his name to the *Kama Sutra*, a work
on erotic techniques. In Hindu marriage rituals a part of the hymns refer to
him. Kama and Rati bring with them the cuckoo, the humming bee, spring and a
gentle breeze.

KRISHNA (India) Krishna is the eighth incarnation of the god Vishnu
and enjoyed many thousands of amorous adventures with women, despite
his enduring love for his consort Radha. He grew up in Brindavan, playing
many pranks, performing miraculous deeds and sporting with *gopis* whom he
charmed with his flute, making them fall madly in love with him. Krishna is
believed to have defeated numerous dragons and monsters, and eventually, as
predicted, killed his half-uncle, the tyrannical king Kamsa. In the epic poem the
Mahabharata, Krishna played a major role that served as the starting point for a
change in Hindu practice. Krishna expounded a philosophy of right action being

---

12 (Hesiod, *Theogony*, 120-2)

the ideal path of salvation, as opposed to relying on ritualistic sacrifices and idol worship. He stated that while yoga and devotion might lead to oneness with God, righteous conduct is better, since it helps in both the spiritual and material worlds.

LIBER (Roman) God of wild places, nature, fertility, wine and passionate sex.

MAPONUS (British) the god of youth and love who corresponds to the Welsh Mabon and the Irish Aengus, and identified with the Roman Apollo. He is also the deity of poetry and music. He was the tutelary god of the Brigantes tribe.

PAN (Greek) The God of fertility, wild places, flocks, animals and male sexuality, lust and love. Pan is the son of the god Hermes by a nymph of Arcadia. The ancient writer Servius described him as being

"Formed in the likeness of nature with horns to resemble the rays of the sun and the horns of the moon; his face is ruddy in the imitation of ether; he wears a spotted fawn skin resembling the stars in the sky; his lower limbs are hairy because of the trees and wild beasts; he has the feet of a goat to resemble the stability of the earth; his pipe has seven reeds in accordance with the harmony of heaven; his pastoral staff bears a crook in reference to the year which curves back on itself, and finally, he is the god of all Nature."

He roams the mountains, pursuing game in the valleys, playing his pipe in the groves and travellers in the woods often hear his music. His call is said to give rise to 'panic', an overwhelming fear in all that hear it.

POTHOS (Greek) Winged god of sexual yearning, love, passion and desire.

Chapter 5
GAY HANDFASTINGS

While the Abrahamic religions condemn homosexuality as a mortal sin, Paganism accepts and honours love and sexuality in all of its many forms as expressions of the Divine. Doreen Valiente's *Charge of the Goddess* states that *"all acts of love and pleasure are my rituals"*. People are created as gay or straight, male or female and dozens of shades between. We may even decide that our spirits were born into a body of the wrong sex and alter that body to fit the real truth of what we are. Homosexuality, bisexuality and transgenderism have always existed. In tribal cultures, both gay people and transsexuals were recognised as special spirits whose unique perspectives brought exceptional vision to the tribe, spirits endowed with a certain "power", or magic, which made them natural intermediaries between the world of the living and realm of the Gods.

Though Paganism, Wicca in particular, works through polarity, we have to remember that we each contain male and female, God and Goddess, within ourselves. My own view is that a coven should represent the whole spectrum of human energy, and should include straight and gay members – our own certainly does.

I am indebted to Wade MacMorrighan for the following material on gay and lesbian weddings:

GAY AND LESBIAN HANDFASTING THEMES
By Wade MacMorrighan

DIVINE TWINS: Anthropologist Will Roscoe (in *Queer Spirits: A Gay Men's Myth Book*) noted a fascinating archetype in the relationships of gay men which he calls "The Divine Twin". When infatuation seems at its height, simultaneous orgasms are common; a lesbian friend once confided to him that when women live together, it's not uncommon for their menses to synchronize; and another example worthy of note, he tells us, is that couples of either gender will find that they

44

start dressing alike, wearing similar-to-identical jewellery, and even having similar/identical tattoos, etc. Roscoe believes that this may be an archetypal manifestation of the Gay bonding process.

THE GREEN MAN/RED MAN (or Holly King/Oak King): One partner could represent the Green Man (spring and summer), while the other embodies the Red Man (autumn and winter). This binomial opposition could reflect and manifest itself in many ways, from Elder/Youth to the notions of balance and equal support: one cannot be without the other.

ASTERION AND THE EARTH-SHAKER (Poseidon): According to the Minoan Brotherhood (a Gay/Bisexual Mens' Wiccan Tradition) a man's lover is revered as the embodiment of the Horned God, specifically Asterion, the starry-bull of heaven. According to their tradition's mythology, Rhea was so in love with Asterion (who represents male ideal beauty) that, out of jealousy, she cursed him never to find love in the arms of a woman; so his cult is thought to have been a homoerotic one. Consequently, his consort is thought to have been the Earth-Shaker (otherwise known as Poseidon). This sacred relationship appears to be reflected in the role of each Grove's High priest and his working partner. The High Priest is referred to as a 'Minos', while his partner, also of the rank of High Priest, is referred to as his 'Server'.

THE HORNED ONE: The Horned God not only represents a father figure, but also embodies an unashamed male sex-drive. Perhaps the theme of two rutting stags (given that homoeroticism exists even in the animal kingdom) would be an interesting theme to reflect upon, or even a ceremony whereby two wands or athames are bound in ceremony.

CUP-BEARER [Father/Son]: One possible archetype in Gay male or Lesbian relationships is the Father-Son Mother-Daughter. This archetype, however, also has its parallels in hetero-centric relationships, such as where a younger spouse chooses to marry a spouse who is their elder or senior, in terms of age relative between that of a parent and child. Amid the Greeks was the notion of *pederasty*, where an older gentleman would notice a male youth in his teenage years; he would then approach the parents of the youth and, if his parents agreed, a ritual abduction told take place, much like Zeus abducting Ganymede. The youth and elder would live together in his house for two months, during which time the youth would be schooled in martial arts. Upon his return, though this is not to say that the relationship was ended or short-lived, the youth brought with him presents for his family (probably a dowry, in reality), such as a suit of armour, ox and a drinking cup, etc.

The cupbearer motif seems to be an Indo-European one with frequently homoerotic themes, for we note Indra and Soma or Agni and Soma, Jupiter and his cupbearer, Ba`al also had a cupbearer, and most famously, Zeus had Ganymede.

DIVINE-LOVERS: There are many male gods who have long-lasting love affairs with other male deities:

*   **Gilgamesh/Enkidu:** Gilgamesh was the king of Uruk who had an insatiable sex-drive. He was besought with dreams that his mother, the wisdom-goddess Ninsun, interpreted to mean that he would soon have a male companion that he would love "as a woman" and would "never forsake" him. The goddess Aruru created, from clay, a male companion for him called Enkidu. Together they journeyed quite happily until Inanna attempted to seduce Enkidu and he refused her offer. This really angered her but her rage was implacable when Enkidu killed her sacred Bull of Heaven. In retaliation, she cursed Enkidu, and he died shortly after. However, it was the loss of his companion that spurred Gilgamesh to discover the secrets of death and rebirth throughout a shamanic underworld quest.

*   **Herakles/Iolaus:** The semi-divine Greek hero Herakles was the son of Zeus. Iolaus was one of his romantic companions associated with shamanistic healing and raising the dead. Iolaus revived his lover after the he had been killed by Typhon, rousing Herakles with the scent of roasted quail. Plutarch commented that male lovers pledge their lives to one another at the tomb and chapel of Iolaus, at Thebes. This complex also had a gymnasium where games, in honour of him, were played; the whole complex was an area where homosexual relationships were consecrated.

*   **Herakles/Hylas:** Another lover of Herakles was Hylas, a beautiful youth and Prince of Thiodamus. He set sail with Herakles and the other Argonauts to adventure. However, when Hylas went in search of water, some seductive nymphs pulled him in and he was drowned. Herakles abandoned the Argonauts to search for Hylas, but in vain. Consequently, in order to celebrate the love between Herakles and Hylas, the people of Chios (now Scio) enacted a ritual drama telling of the search for Hylas.

*   **Hyacynthus/Apollon:** Hyacynthus was a Spartan Prince (hence would have been a hard-bodied warrior and military leader, rather than an effeminate lily-

46

prince, as so often depicted). He was accidentally killed by his lover Apollo when an errant discus struck him in the face. As a result, Apollo turned him into the flower which is marked with his grief. Hyacynthus was a dying-and-rising god who was celebrated during a festival in his honour; his tomb was also reputed to be at the foot of Apollo's Temple. Perhaps this symbolizes the eternal love that transcends death.

* **Vishnu/Shiva:** In Hindu Epic, two very potent gods who came together in a night of passion (albeit Shiva is in drag at the time, and going by the "drag"– name of Mohini) giving rise to the birth of the god, Harihara (the guardian of highways, sharing aspects with both his male parents).

WARRIOR-LOVERS: Greek heroes and semi-divine heroes also litter the historical record with their love of men roughly of the same age. The Sacred Band of Thebes during the fourth-century BCE comprised a battalion of 300 paired warrior-lovers from the Greek city-state of Thebes which eventually succumbed to the onslaught of Philip of Macedon and Alexander the Great during the Battle of Chaeronea in 338. Philip, who wanted to unify the Greek city-states under his rule in order to invade Persia, saw them as an obstacle to his political ambitions when they mounted a revolt in opposition to his personal agenda. It was a common custom among Greek occupied legions to be particularly devoted to Eros in the belief that military success was best won because a lover would rather die in battle than be disgraced as a coward in the eyes of their belovéd – a Platonic philosophy that was adopted, for example, by the Thebans and the Lacedaemonians, as well as the Athenian armed-forces. Greek soldiers habitually sacrificed to Eros before entering into battle. After all, no Gay man comes through this life without scars; we are fighters, soldiers, and survivors with the battle marks to prove it! We are a "band of brothers"; we are kin.

These contain a theme I believe important for many lovers, whether that couple be male or female: it could serve as a useful metaphor for living, at times, in an unkindly world that has harmed Gay men and Lesbians in the past or present; to defending the honour of one's lover when insulted; to entering the battlefield of love to find that special someone.

* **Achilles and Patroclus:** Achilles, the semi-divine hero had a comrade-lover called Patroclus. When Patroclus was killed, his spirit quickly appeared to Achilles, begging him to get on with his funerary rites so that he might have rest as soon as possible. Later on, however, when Achilles met his own tragic end, they appear to have been reburied together in a single grave. The goddess

Thetis, Achilles' mother, kept their bones with her at all times, mixed together in a golden urn.

* **Antheus:** A Trojan warrior who was the lover of Paris and his brother Deiphobus, both Trojan Princes.

* **Aravan:** A Hindu god-hero, the son of Arjuna. When it was decreed by one Sahadev that, in order to win the battle of Kurukshetra, Arjuna or Krishna would have to offer up his own life, Aravan stepped in to take their place, but, the night before he was beheaded, Krishna took the form of a woman and married him, so that he might first know the love of a woman. After Aravan's death, Krishna remained in female form for a time as a grieving widow. The love between Krishna and Aravan is commemorated annually in the town of Koovagam by the Hijra priest/ess (who have undergone a partial sex-change operation; it is believed that they have the power to curse a man with impotence should he desecrate them, despite the fact that they are a despised class of Indian society). At these rituals the Hijras take on the role of Krishna as bride, and a priest ties a *thali* around their necks (this is a cord or thread covered in turmeric, which is a yellow dye herb), which is meant to symbolize their marriage to Aravan.

* **Baton ["Blackberry"]/Amphiaraus:** Baton was the latter's lover and charioteer. Just as they were about to be struck and killed by some enemy, Zeus caused the Earth to open up and swallow them until danger had passed which seems to be a death and rebirth sequence. Baton had a cult at Argos where he was revered as a deified warrior. Amphiaraus was regarded as an oracle and founded an incubation chamber/temple at Oropus where parishioners would come to sleep and have their dreams interpreted. After his death funeral games were established in his honour.

* **Cú Chullain/Fer Diadh:** Cú was a semi-divine hero, and Fer was his foster-brother. Together they were trained in the martial arts under the tutelage of the goddess, Scathach ["Shade"]. They were forced to fight together on the whim of Queen Maeve who was the ultimate instigator of the *Táin*. Fer, not wishing to fight his foster-brother says of their relationship, *"Fast friends, forest companions/ We made one bed and slept one sleep."* They were forced to battle anyway. After the end of the first day, however, they found one another, kissed, and traded food as well as herbal medicine, and even placed their horses in the same stable. While they could not sleep near each other, their charioteers did. This pattern repeated itself for three days, when, on the forth day, Cú killed

Fer. After which, he cradled his body and lamented for him, perhaps much like Achilles and Apollo for their lovers.

LESBIAN UNIONS

Poets spoke of lesbian relationships metaphorically as the "Praiser" and the "Praised". Lesbian rites in the Classical world seemed to have primarily taken place during the rising of the Pleiades (known as the "Seven Sisters") or at at the rising of the Dog Star, Sirius. Afterwards, while these women usually married a man, this was by no means universal.

They were solemnized with the invocation or patronage of such dawn-goddesses as Aotis, while Aurora was apparently regarded as the patron of unions between two women and was worshipped by members of the Thiasos of Sappho on the Island of Lesbos. The importance of these deities of dawn is probably because these rites began at dawn, and ended at dusk. Other deities invoked, particularly during Lesbian rites of union, were Artemis Orthia and Artemis Pergaea, Aphrodite, Helen of Troy, the Graces, Eros and Apollo.

The couple would have worn garments of red [sacred to Aphrodite,] and purple [sacred to Eros]. On the altar it is likely that roses, anise, hyacinth and wildflowers will have been placed, along with a censor with frankincense. These were generally recorded for the worship of Aphrodite by Sappho. The most symbolic and important element was an image of a plough, which probably represented erotic symbolism (i.e. "ploughing the earth"), and the couple's *syzygos*, meaning "to yoke together". Ritual food was served, including apples, honey and probably cakes in the shape of breasts. Many hymns were sung addressing the couple, employing metaphors likening the couple to horses, the Pleiades and even Sirius.

MORE DEITIES FOR GAY AND LESBIAN HANDFASTINGS

BEC: A Celtic warrioress who was the intimate companion of Lithben. It is thought that they may have been members of an 'Amazonian' Celtic battalion.

EROS: Eros ("sexual desire") was initially the divine personification of order in Greek cosmogony, i.e. he was the drive that fashioned form and substance from disparate matter. According to Hesiod's *Theogony*, Eros was born of Chaos and was the first among the pre-Olympian deities, the "Force" that set the Universe in motion. Conversely, he was also conceived of as *"the dissolver of flesh, who overcomes the reason and the purpose in the breasts of all gods and all men"*, thus illustrating that he was – and is – the most powerful of the pre-Olympian gods. It was only later that

49

Greek mythographers made him the son and constant attendant of Aphrodite and fathered by Hermes, Ares or Zeus. However, according to the Orphic account of his birth he sprang from the Cosmic Egg, the progeny of black-winged Night (Nyx), from whose broken shell was formed the Earth (Gaea) and the Heavens (Uranus).

The Hellenistic Eros was Desire – not in the courtly Christian expression of "love", but the personification of our innate erotic impulses. Moreover, he may have been a phallic-deity, the manifestation of a male's arousal function. He was armed with a bow and a quiver of gold or lead-tipped arrows that he sharpened on a grindstone whetted with blood. While a gold-tipped arrow would enflame body and soul with passion for another individual, a lead-tipped arrow would cause aversion towards the would be lover, perhaps as punishment for transgressions against the god.

During the Classical period, Eros was regarded as the particular patron for homo-erotically inclined men. In gymnasia – where his idol stood – he bestowed the blessing of physical beauty onto male lovers, forming one facet of a "homoerotic trinity" alongside Hermes (who bestowed lovers with the gift of eloquence) and Herakles (who offered strength to male sexual partners). Indeed, his idol is frequently housed in such male dominated institutions as gymnasia, wrestling schools and military training academies. Moreover, he was responsible for the sexual education of young men, perhaps alongside Athena (goddess of wisdom and warfare) with whom he was occasionally paired.

Men living in ancient Greece (and out-lying territories) were expected to be "confirmed bachelors" usually until their thirties or forties, when the most dangerous period of military service had passed. Endorsed homosexuality allowed men to deal with their sexual impulses. However, loving homosexual relationships were not strictly limited to those between an older man and an adolescent (*pederasty*), but were also documented among young men of similar age range (for example, in late teenage years), even culminating in devotional poems and love letters as an expression of those romantic feelings.

ZEPHYRUS (Greek) the god of the wind who was jealous of Apollo's love for the youth Hyacinthus and the time they spent together. One day, Apollo and Hyacinthus were playing quoits. Apollo threw a disc, but Zephyrus blew it off course, and it struck the boy's head, killing him. Distraught that he had killed his friend, Apollo turned him into a flower.

HYACINTHUS (Greek) See above.

APOLLO (Greek) the god of the sun, healing, poetry and divination, Apollo

50

seems to have been attracted to both male and female lovers. For one tale of his love for a youth see Zephyrus above.

GANYMEDE (Greek) a youthful prince of Troy who caught the eye of Zeus, the king of the gods who took the shape of an eagle to seize the boy and carry him to Olympus, where he acted as his cup bearer. His jealous wife Hera insisted the Zeus send the boy away and he eventually agreed, but first made him immortal, setting him in the stars as the constellation of Aquarius.

CATAMITUS (Roman) – a beautiful youth loved by Jupiter, in a parallel tale to the story of Ganymede and Zeus. The word 'catamite' used to be used to describe gay men.

HARIHARA (Hindu) a god born of the union of the male deities, Shiva and Vishnu. His name means "Golden Ravisher" and he is shown with Vishnu occupying the female, left half of his body and Shiva the male, right half. He is the guardian of highways who may bring or take away blight.

ARDHANARISHVARA, (Hindu) a deity, half-man and half-woman, with the right side representing Shiva and the left side Parvati. The male side wears a leopard skin and has a serpent coiling around his arm, while the female side wears an orange skirt, a scarf and plenty of jewellery.

DIANA (Roman) – maiden goddess of the moon and hunt, armed with crescent moon bow and arrows, a personification of Nature, roaming through the moonlit wilds, followed by her dancing nymph disciples. Late Roman sources and the inquisitors of the Middle Ages described her as the leader of the witches.

ARTEMIS (Greek) the daughter of Zeus, King of the Greek gods, and Leto, one of his many mistresses. She was worshipped by the warrior Amazons as new moon goddess. When Artemis was a little girl, Zeus, her father, wanted to give her a gift and asked her what she wanted. The goddess replied "I want to run forever wild and free with my hounds in the woods and never, ever marry". Those men who defiled her mysteries she ruthlessly hunted down and killed. When women married, they had to leave her service forever. Artemis is the goddess that women call upon when they are in trouble or abused. She befriends the abused and punishes the abuser. Within every woman the spirit of Artemis exists, independent, confident. She doesn't deny her own nature to satisfy another.

Rose (*Rosa* spp.): One of the sacred symbols of Eros. Idols of Cupid were frequently crowned with chaplets of roses throughout Rome.

Myrtle: This tree was dedicated to the god Hesperus who presided over Ceremonies of Union during the evening, and who took the god Hymenaeus as his lover. Hymenaeus was reputed to sing hymns at Union Ceremonies (probably for all couples, regardless of gender).

Poppy and Anise: These two herbs were named, respectively, after two Roman youths (Papaver and Anethus) who were either loved by male gods, or loved each other. Upon dying, each was transformed into his name-sake, and for this reason, poppies and anise form one of the garland plants given to a man's lover. During rites of Lesbian union, anise was incorporated into the chaplet.

Roses and Violets: Neck garlands of these flowers were worn by the couple during Lesbian union rituals.

Chapter 6
CHOOSING THE MOMENT

As a Pagan, you will want to choose the most auspicious moment for your handfasting. Magicians believe that there are tides of waxing and waning energies concerned with the phases of the moon, position of the planets and the time of year. Begin a venture when the energies are waning, and you are swimming against the tide of power and you will find that difficulties and obstacles strew your path. Begin when the energies are waxing or full, and everything will flow more easily, and you are more likely to succeed. Handfasting is one of the most important magical rites that you will ever engage in, just as the choosing of a partner is one of the most crucial decisions of your life.

ACCORDING TO THE PHASE OF THE MOON

Witches practice magic according to the phases of the moon. The moon was the earliest method of measuring the passage of time. Its waxing and waning marked off the days, and the root word for moon still gives us our words for month, measurement and menstruation. While the moon is a constant presence in the night sky it is ever changing. Women often feel an identity with the moon; the menstrual cycles begins in youth and the womb waxes and wanes, bleeding each month until the onset of the menopause and the belly swells like a full moon during pregnancy. So, the phases of the moon can be seen as reflected in the life of women and the ever present but ever changing Great Goddess herself: the waxing moon as maiden; full moon as pregnant mother and the waning moon as Queen and dark moon as hag.

From the moon we learn that each thing has its season- a time to be born, a time to grow, a time to wither, and a time to end and pass back into the void- only to return again. It is important to recognise the time for an idea, project or relationship to be born, the time to bring it to maturity and the time to let go of it. Everything will change and come again in its season, changeless, moving and flowing.

People often speak of the three phases of the moon, but it actually has four – three visible (waxing, full and waning) then three days in darkness.

Waxing Moon

The waxing (growing) moon is a good time for starting new projects, new relationships and for planting flowers and vegetables. It is a time for beginnings, things that will grow to fullness in the future. The waxing moon may be a lucky time for a handfasting, and represents your hopes for what is yet to come.

Full Moon

The full moon is a good time for positive magic – healing, blessing and so on. It is a very creative period and you will feel the benefit when working on imaginative projects such as writing, painting or composing music. The energy of the full moon celebrates the fertile, positive, creative forces in the world and in relationships and is a good time for a handfasting.

Waning Moon

The waning (shrinking) moon is a time for letting go of bad habits, negative thinking etc. It is a time of winding down, relinquishing old relationships and situations. It is the time to perform purifications and cleansing magic, for handparting – the ending of a relationship, rather than a handfasting.

The Dark Moon

During the three days of dark moon the moon regenerates itself and began life anew, just as all life generates in the darkness of the womb or seeds in the dark earth, growing to maturity in the light. The days of the dark moon are good for deep inner journeys and meditations rather than the outward expression of the life journey. During this dark phase, the moon somehow regenerates itself and begins life anew, just as all life generates in the darkness of the womb or seeds in the dark earth, growing to maturity in the light before ageing and dying and returning to the darkness where life begins again, month after month, season after season, year after year. This is not really suitable for a handfasting.

TIME OF DAY

I once went to a handfasting held at Handfast Point, a cliff overlooking the sea in the south of England. It was held at dawn as the sun came up, a powerful symbol of new beginnings. However, it might mean more to you to be married at midday, representing the zenith of the day's power, or at dusk, when the Otherworld becomes close. Maybe you would like to marry at the witching hour of midnight, or at the time you first met. Choose the symbolism that is right for you and your relationship.

ACCORDING TO THE SABBAT

The eight Pagan Sabbats of witches represent the waxing and waning of the solar year. Though the feminine energy of the Goddess is present throughout the cycle, the power of the God ebbs and flows throughout the year. The eight Sabbats mark his life cycle. He is born at the winter solstice, is nursed at Imbolc, grows to manhood at Ostara, marries the Goddess at Beltane, fertilises her at Midsummer, is honoured as high king at Lughnasa, sacrifices himself for the greater good at Herfest (the autumn equinox), rules the land of the dead at Samhain and comes to rebirth at Yule.

As the summer sun, he brings fertility, sexual power and fruitfulness. The mating of the sun and earth brings about the flowering and fruiting of Mother Earth.

Candlemas/Imbolc (*'in the belly'*) celebrates the first stirrings of spring, around 2nd February. This is a festival of the waxing year, when the sun is growing stronger, the days longer, and the first shoots force their way through the frozen earth. New lambs are born are born in the fields and ewes come into milk, a symbol of purity and nurturing, respectively. The festival is dedicated to the maiden goddess of spring, and some consider it inappropriate for a handfasting. However, in Celtic myth it is dedicated to the triple goddess Brighid or Bride, perhaps the origin of our word 'bride', so others think it entirely appropriate. During this time the young god moves through childhood and approaches puberty.

Ostara celebrates the vernal equinox, spring and the growing light, around 21st March. Wiccans see this as the time when the young God and Goddess meet as youth and maid. It is a lucky time for a wedding, with vital life burgeoning throughout nature. Leaves unfurl on the trees, sun coloured daffodils bloom in the hedgerows, and animals prepare nests, ready for mating.

Beltane (*'bright-fire'*) marks the start of summer and fertility around May 1st. May has been considered an unlucky month in which to marry in for a number of reasons. This season was considered to be the time of the sacred marriage of the Gods, and was therefore taboo for human weddings. Beltane is a festival of death, as well as rebirth, the death of winter and birth of summer. Though Bel is a god of summer fire, he is also the winter ruler of the dead. In ancient Rome the Feast of the Dead and the festival of the goddess of chastity both occurred in May, neither appropriate times to hold a wedding. However, many modern witches and Pagans see this as a fortuitous time for handfasting with the flowering of the year.

Coamhain/Midsummer is the time of the summer solstice, the zenith of the sun and summer around 21st June the month of June is a traditionally lucky time for weddings, as it is sacred to (and named after) Juno, the Roman goddess of marriage.

Lughnasa/Lammas-the beginning of the harvest, the prime of the corn Lord, around 2nd August. This was the traditional time for handfastings among the ancients, carried out at the annual clan gatherings or fairs.

The Autumn Equinox/Herfest celebrates the autumn equinox, the harvest festival, death of the Corn Lord, waning of the sun, around 21st September. From this point in the cycle until Yule, the Lord is absent from the cycle, so this is not a good time for a marriage.

Samhain – the start of winter, festival of the dead, around 31st October, the contracting energies of Samhain are concerned with dissolution, death, winter, and the spirits of the ancestors. For Wiccans, this is the time when the god rules as Lord of the Dead in the Underworld, lying in the earth-womb of the goddess. This is not a lucky time for a wedding.

Yule – the winter solstice, the rebirth of the sun, around 21st December and the start of the waxing year. This is the time when the God is reborn and energy flows back into the world. It is a good festival on which to celebrate a handfasting.

Though it might not be appropriate to marry on a Sabbat associated with waning sun energies, if you cannot wait for the next appropriate Sabbat, you might choose another day in the same month, on a waxing or full moon.

ACCORDING TO THE MONTH

Some of the ancient Pagan beliefs found their way into popular wedding lore in more recent times. Victorian brides were warned '*Marry in the month of May, and you'll live to rue the day*' an old taboo from Pagan times. Even Queen Victoria prevented her children from marrying in May, and April 30th was a busy time for vicars, with brides trying to marry before the May prohibition began. An old rhyme states:

- Married when the year is new, he'll be loving, kind & true.
- When February birds do mate, you wed nor dread your fate.
- If you wed when March winds blow, joy and sorrow both you'll know.
- Marry in April when you can, joy for Maiden and for Man.
- Marry in the month of May, and you'll surely rue the day.
- Marry when June roses grow, over land and sea you'll go.
- Those who in July do wed, must labour for their daily bread.
- Whoever wed in August be, many a change is sure to see.
- Marry in September's shrine, your living will be rich and fine.
- If in October you do marry, love will come but riches tarry.
- If you wed in bleak November, only joys will come, remember.
- When December snows fall fast, marry and true love will last.

Remember that the above is just Victorian whimsy, and I have only included it for fun. It has little basis in real magical lore.

ACCORDING TO THE DAYS OF THE WEEK
According to an old English rhyme, different days of the week are lucky or unlucky for weddings:

> *Monday for wealth*
> *Tuesday for health*
> *Wednesday the best day of all*
> *Thursday for losses*
> *Friday for crosses*
> *Saturday for no luck at all*

The favourite day on which to be married was Sunday, until the Puritans made this illegal. The unluckiest day of all was Saturday, the very time when most weddings take place today. This may be because it is the day of Saturn, the planet which is concerned with endings, dissolution and death. Friday was also considered unlucky amongst Christians, as Christ was crucified on a Friday, though for Pagans Friday is the day of Venus, the planet of love, sacred in ancient times to the ancient Goddess of Love in her various guises. She is always associated with the sea, and it is for this reason that fish was eaten on a Friday, a custom later adopted by Christians.

You can take the planetary rulers of the days into account:

SUNDAY – (ruled by the Sun) rules employers, friendship, healing and work, it is named after the sun and is sacred to the Sun God who rules fertility, passion and sexual energy.

MONDAY – **(ruled by the Moon)** rules agriculture, psychic ability, witchcraft, the home and medicine, it is named after the moon and is sacred to the Moon Goddess who rules fertility, feminine power and the emotions, including love.

TUESDAY – **(ruled by the planet Mars)** rules conflict, competition, debates, courage and lust, it is named after the Norse war god Tiw.

WEDNESDAY – **(ruled by the planet Mercury)** rules study, teaching, divination and communications, it is named after the northern chief god Woden who rules expansive energies, bards and divination.

THURSDAY – **(ruled by the planet Jupiter)** rules material things, money, property and luck, it is named after the northern storm god Thor.

FRIDAY – **(ruled by the planet Venus)** rules love, art, music, incense and perfume making, it is named after Freya or Frigg, the northern Goddess of Love.

SATURDAY – **(ruled by the planet Saturn)** rules the elderly, death, re-incarnation, wills, destruction, death and endings, it is named after the Roman god Saturn.

Chapter 7
HANDFASTING THEMES

There is no need to theme your handfasting or elaborate the proceedings in any way, but you might like to include traditions and costumes from your cultural heritage, or explore meaningful Pagan symbolism in your ceremony. Marriage traditions from around the world offer a fascinating array of customs you might want to include.

SIMPLE PAGAN
The ritual of handfasting does not need to be complicated or expensive; its purpose is for the couple to declare their intentions in front of witnesses and the Old Gods. You might make a simple circle of flowers or crystals in your house or in an open space, invite friends and family to be present and follow the ceremony with a celebratory meal for which everyone brings food and drink to share. This can be the loveliest handfasting of all. Some simple Pagan handfasting rites are given in the Rituals Chapter.

FORMAL WICCAN
For the Wiccan, the handfasting is usually a formal ritual held in front of the entire coven. Non Wiccans may watch from outside the circle (or inside if they and your high priestess agrees). Participants are robed, with the bride and groom wearing coloured robes for the occasion (the traditional colour for the bride is red) and wearing chaplets of flowers and ivy. Sometimes coloured sashes are worn. The Wiccan handfasting rite is given in the Rituals Chapter.

AS SUN AND MOON
You might like to explore the symbolism of the marriage of the God and Goddess as sun and moon, and dress the circle and participants accordingly. The groom would dress in gold, and wear symbols of the sun, with crystals such as amber, topaz and tiger eye. The bride might wear silver for the moon, and adorn

her brow with a crescent moon and wear gems such as moonstones, pearls or opals. The time for this wedding would be Beltane, Midsummer, Yule, full moon or waxing moon for preference.

AS SKY AND EARTH

The God and Goddess also represent the sky and the earth respectively. It is the fertilising rain of the sky father that causes the earth mother to flower and bring forth grain. Again, you might explore the symbolism of this in your ritual, with the groom dressed in blue and wearing sun and lightening/thunder symbols, and the bride in green and adorned with flowers and grain. The best time for this would be Ostara, Beltane, Midsummer or Lughnasa.

ROMAN

If you worship the Roman gods, are of Italian ancestry, or just very interested in the ancient Romans, then you might like incorporate some of the customs of an ancient Roman wedding into your handfasting. The bride was attended by a matron of honour and the groom by a best man who also acted as priest. The bride prepared for the wedding by symbolically renouncing her childhood by giving up her childish toys and maiden's dress (even if the bride isn't a young maiden, some of the imagery of this might be employed).

The ceremony largely revolved round the veiling of the bride and the term describing a married woman *nupta* means 'I veil myself'. The wedding was called the *nuptiae* and from this we get our modern word 'nuptials'. She wore a long, flame coloured transparent veil called a *flammeum*, which was secured by a wreath. Unlike the modern bridal veil, it did not cover up her face. She also wore a white tunic fastened by a girdle, which the groom had the fun of untying on the wedding night. Her hair was divided into six strands, fastened with fillets on top of her head in a cone. During the styling, the hair was parted with a bent iron spearhead to drive evil spirits from her.

The bride's parents handed her over to the groom with some exchange of vows (you can write your own). The matron of honour would then join the couple's hands. They would make an offering to the gods together and the contract was signed by witnesses. The *cena*, or wedding breakfast, followed during which gifts would be given to the happy couple.

Then ensued the wedding procession from the bride's home to the groom's, consisting of the bride, groom, three male attendants and other guests, beginning with a representational seizing of the bride from her mother's arms by the groom. Guests would make the kind of suggestive jokes and comments that are still made at weddings today. One of the male attendants would carry a torch lit from the bride's hearth which would be used to light a fire at her new home.

Walnuts were thrown at the couple as a fertility ritual. The bride carried a distaff or spindle. At some point the procession split so that the groom could hurry to his house in order to be there first to greet the bride.

When the procession arrived at the house, the torches were thrown away, and the bride rubbed the doorway with fat and oil and wreathed it with wool. She was carried over the threshold so that she should not trip, which would be unlucky. She then touched water and fire. Inside was a miniature marriage bed for the spirits of the bride and groom to consummate their joining. Songs were then sung to encourage the couple to consummate the marriage in a chamber decorated with fertility symbols, greenery and fruit. The matron of honour, a married woman herself, led the bride into it and wished the couple perpetual harmony.

SAXON
Very little is known about the customs of Saxon marriages. Taticus, writing of *Germania*, says that brides were obtained by payment of a dowry by the groom in the form of sword and shield, cattle and bridled horse. On the morning after the wedding, the groom also had to give his new wife a morning gift, the *morgengifu*. This was hers to keep and use the entirety of her life. This lack of information gives you plenty of scope to design your own Saxon style handfasting. It is sure to include plenty of ale, mead and feasting.

VIKING
Viking weddings were traditionally held on a Friday, the day sacred to Freya or Frigga, the Goddess of Love. Ceremonies often lasted for a week or more, and included the drinking of a special bridal ale, brewed with honey. The bride and groom drank this for the following month, a period called the honey moon, and this is where we get the word from.

Before the wedding the bride was purified by her attendants in a ritual bath, dressed in a gown, a blue cloak and the bridal crown, woven from corn and flowers. The groom also underwent a ritual bath and was instructed by the older, married men, on his duties as a husband and father, and given advice. He dressed in his best clothes and wore his ancestral sword.

On the wedding day, the dowries were exchanged and the wedding took place at an open air site. The bride was accompanied by a young kinsman bearing a new sword as a present for her husband. The gods were invoked and honoured with offerings. The groom then presented the bride with the sword of his ancestors to be held in trust by her for their descendants, symbolising the family line, protection and tradition. She then gave him the new sword so that he might protect her and their future family with it. The couple then exchanged rings, with the bride's ring offered to her on the hilt of her husband's new sword. They then both placed their hands on the sword hilt and exchanged vows.

Afterwards there was a race or 'bride running' to the feasting hall. The last party there may have had to serve the others at the feast. [13]

MEDIAEVAL

A mediaeval theme to handfasting is becoming increasingly popular, as many venues offer mediaeval-type banquets and entertainment. In mediaeval times, the rich enjoyed sumptuous weddings, with enormous feasts and jousting contests.

The bride may wear a long gown with wide sleeves with a veil fixed by a fillet of silver, or a wreath of flowers. The groom may dress in doublet and hose, and the colours of male and female attire were often matched, the most prestigious colours being purple, crimson and royal blue, expensive dyes that only the rich could afford. Both men and women wore ribbons tied around their arms or pinned to their costumes. Men wore small posies of herbs pinned to their doublets, and the bridesmaids carried nosegays of scented herbs and flowers. The bride might have sprigs of rosemary in her bouquet or in her bridal wreath. At her wedding to Henry VIII in 1540, Anne of Cleves wore a gold coronet encircled with sprigs of rosemary. Records tell us that some medieval brides carried a little bouquet of gilded marigolds that were dipped in rosewater. The marigolds were thought to have aphrodisiac qualities and were eaten after the ceremony.

To reinforce the Mediaeval theme, use heraldic banners, metal goblets and candles on tall iron sconces. If the event or wedding feast takes place indoors, decorate with banners, ivy, flowers and weaponry such as swords, axes and so on. You can use recorded music or hire minstrels to serenade you with lute and pipes.

SCOTTISH

In Scotland it was traditional for the Bride to 'walk with the sun', circling the Church three times 'sunwise' for good luck. This undoubtedly dates from an older Pagan tradition in which she walked three times deosil round the sacred circle or holy ground in an act of positive magic.

The rings could be engraved with the words *Mo ghaol ort* or "I love you" in Scots Gaelic. The bride might wear a traditional Luckenbooth brooch, a pin of engraved silver in the shape of a heart or two hearts entwined which is given to her by the groom. Afterwards this brooch is pinned to the blanket of their first child for luck. A must for the bride, groom and guests is the lucky white heather.

---

13   Gunnora Hallakarva, http://www.drizzle.com/~celyn/mrwp/vikwed5.txt

A traditional wedding blessing is:
"A thousand welcomes to you with your marriage kerchief,
may you be healthy all your days.
May you be blessed with long life and peace,
May you grow old with goodness and with riches."

IRISH

Lady Wilde described an old rustic Irish wedding witnessed by a traveller in Kerry in the early eighteen hundreds, which seems very Pagan in character.[14] It took place under a hawthorn tree which was decorated with ribbons and rush candles among the branches. A procession of boys marching slowly with flutes, reed pipes, a tin drum and bone rattles processed to the tree, followed by a boy with a blazing torch, and behind him the couple hand in hand. A canopy of dark cloth was held over them, and two attendants held over their heads a sieve filled with meal, obviously a fertility charm to ensure plenty in their future lives. The guests followed singing and dancing and waving green leafy branches. The procession moved to the bonfire and circled it three times, then the black cloth was lifted from over the bridal pair, and they kissed each other, while the guests applauded and cheered, waving their branches. This was followed by feasting and drinking, and no doubt, the party lasted all night. Food might include Irish soda bread, champ (mashed potatoes with spring onions), and fruit cake with almonds, raisins, cherries and spice. There should be plenty of whiskey and Guinness to drink.

On arriving at her future home, the bride was met on the threshold by her bridegroom 's mother, who broke an oaten cake over her head a good augury of plenty in the future.

You might have the rings engraved with *A rún mo chroí,* which translates as "Oh love of my heart" or *A mhuirnín dílis* meaning "Oh true sweetheart".

ROMANY

The gypsy woman wears red on her wedding day as a symbol that she is still a virgin. The *abiav* or wedding has little religious content, and its customs vary from region to region. Often no formal ritual is necessary, and the couple just agree to live together in front of witnesses, joining hands in the presence of the chief of the tribe or other elder. Some celebrate by placing a drop of their blood on some bread and each eating the other's. Alternatively, bread and salt is placed on the knees of the seated bride. The groom then takes some of the bread and dips it into the salt before eating it.

14   Ancient Legends, *Mystic Charms and Superstitions of Ireland.*, Ticknor and Co., Boston, 1887.

INDIA

In a custom reminiscent of a western stag night, the groom spends his last night of freedom with his male friends. They eat a meal and perform a ritual purification of the groom by pouring water from a jug over him. Turmeric paste (a yellow spice) is rubbed on to his face and chest to give him a sunny glow which wards off evil spirits. The bride is painted with elaborate henna patterns by her attendants. At the ceremony, the groom's brother sprinkles flower petals over the couple and a coconut, representing fertility is held over their heads and circled three times.

SERBIA

The groom's father issues the wedding invitations by going from house to house with a flask of brandy. Guests are invited to toast the couple and give the messenger a small present for his trouble. On the wedding morning the best man must retrieve a gourd and a handkerchief from the top of a tree before the groom is allowed to enter the bride's house.

JEWISH

The bride and groom clasp hands as a sign of their bond. The groom gives the celebrant a handkerchief containing six coins which he hands over to the bride's father as a symbolic bride price. The couple drink from a glass which is then broken as a sign that what has been done cannot be undone.

CHINA

In China red is the lucky colour, so the bridal dress, the invitations and even the sheets on the marriage bed are red. Red candles and lamps may also be used. Rice wine is traditional. Chinese brides receive presents of gold jewellery from their female relatives.

DENMARK

As soon as the groom is alone, all the women at the celebration try to kiss him. When he leaves the room, all the men try to steal kisses from the bride. In a dance, the groom's relatives circle him and cut up his tie. The traditional wedding cake is the cornucopia of almond and marzipan decorated with marzipan portraits of the bride and groom.

TURKEY

After the wedding ceremony, the couple must remain apart for twenty four hours, and then the groom must run the gauntlet to the room where his love awaits, while his friends throw old shoes at him. The bride and groom then share some sugar as a sign of the sweetness to come.

PHILLIPINES
A white silk cord is placed around the couple's shoulders to indicate their union. At some point in the ceremony white doves are released to symbolise peace and happiness for the bride and groom in their new lives.

YUGOSLAVIA
One old ceremony in the former Yugoslavia consisted of a torchlight procession which accompanied a young girl to three fountains. She had to take a mouthful of water from one, and carry it to the next and so on. At the last she carried the water in her mouth back to the bride's home, where she spat it into a jug which was used for the bride's ritual purification.

AFRICA
Sew some cowrie shells into your wedding costume to symbolise, fertility, beauty, purification, wealth and power. The ancestors are invited to be present and a libation is poured as an offering to them. Fill a cup with water and explain that you are pouring it on the ground, in the north, east, south and west, to honour your ancestors. Water is the source of life and its nourishment, used for purification and to symbolise the sustenance of the spirit.

ARMENIA
The bride dresses in red silk and has feathered wings as a headdress. The guests throw coins at her.

BELGIUM
The bride embroiders her name on a handkerchief and carries it on her wedding day, then frames it.

BERMUDA
The wedding cake is topped with a sapling tree. The couple plant this in their garden and watch it grow as their relationship develops.

BOHEMIA
The groom gives the bride a girdle with three keys, a fur cap, and a silver wedding ring. She gives him an embroidered shirt and a wedding ring. The best man wraps the groom in the bride's cloak to keep evil spirits from getting between the couple and causing trouble.

CROATIA

After the ceremony, the bride's veil is removed by the married women present, and replaced with an apron and headscarf to show her new status. They then sing to her and she has to walk three times around the well and throw three apples into it for fertility.

CZECHOSLOVAKIA

Friends plant a tree in the bride's garden and decorate it with painted eggs and ribbons. This is a symbol of fertility, and it is said that the bride will live as long as the tree.

ENGLAND

In times past, the bride's party walked to the church led by a girl strewing petals on the road, symbolising a sweet path for the bride. She carried a lucky horseshoe, though nowadays these are made of silver or cardboard. Then she must have *"Something Old, Something New, Something Borrowed, Something Blue, and a Silver Sixpence in her Shoe"* according to a Victorian rhyme. Something old represents continuity with the past, something new is a token of her new future and altered status, something borrowed is a token of friendship, and blue was the colour of the Goddess in ancient times, though many modern brides do not realise why they have to wear blue! The silver sixpence in the shoe represents wealth and plenty. Now sixpences are no longer made, the bride has to be content with a silver five pence piece, unless the family have an old sixpence lying around somewhere. If you find a spider in your wedding dress, this is very lucky.

FINLAND

The bride wears a golden crown, which later on she must place on another's head while blindfolded. Whoever is crowned will be the next to marry. At the reception, the bride holds a sieve covered with a shawl and the guests put presents of money into it.

FRANCE

Many couples drink the bridal toast from the *coupe de marriage*, a two handled loving cup.

MODERN GREECE

Today, the *koumbaros* or best man places crowns of white or gold (or perhaps made of flowers, or twigs and vine wrapped in silver paper) on the heads of the couple. To ensure a sweet life, the bride carries some sugar.

ANCIENT EGYPT

The ancient Egyptians were probably the first to have laws covering marriage, which they considered to be both a spiritual and legal arrangement. The laws covered the rights and duties of the couple, including the right of divorce for both men and women. Marriage contracts were signed by three witnesses and included the name of the couple, the names of both sets of parents, the profession of husband and wife, and the signature of the scribe who drew up the contract, plus details of any settlement- a pre-nuptial agreement- to be made in the case of divorce. The contract was then kept at the temple. Sometimes a trial marriage was agreed upon, to see whether the wife or husband were fertile and it was sometimes stipulated in the pre-nuptial contract that the marriage would end if pregnancy did not ensue with a year. Though the Egyptians have left no records of a formal marriage ceremony, it is known that they held a wedding party with the bride probably dressed in her best linen tunic and finest jewellery. Then the bride moved to her husband's house, taking all her belongings with her.

NATIVE AMERICAN

Many Native American groups traditionally formalised marriage by gift exchanges between the bride and groom's families. The bride's family would give "women's things" such as beadwork, baskets, cloth and cooking utensils, while the groom's family would give "men's things" like knives, hides, guns, horses and blankets.

ANCIENT GREECE

In ancient Athens the favourite month for marriage was *Gamelion*, or January, since it was sacred to Hera, the goddess of marriage. The celebrations preferably took place at the full moon. After a formal betrothal ceremony which dealt with the legal aspects of the marriage, the wedding itself took place a few days later. The bride dedicated her childish toys and girl's tunic to Artemis the maiden goddess, to show that her childhood was over. Then she dressed in her finest clothes and veil, and went down to party gathered at her father's house where the groom and his best man or *paranymphos* was waiting. A lamb was eaten, and everyone shared a large flat cake of pounded sesame seeds roasted and mixed with honey. Then at some point in the evening, the bride's mother handed her over to the groom who took her away in his chariot. He and the best man sat either side of her as they processed to his house singing the marriage song *"Ho, Hymen! Ho, Hymen! Hymenæous! Io!"* while onlookers wished them well. At the groom's house they were showed with confetti, and the bride had to stop on the threshold to eat a quince, a symbol of fertility. While the groom's friends continued to party, the bride was led, still veiled, to the flower bedecked bridal chamber, where she was joined by the groom.

HOLLAND
The bride and groom sit on thrones under a canopy of evergreens as the guests take turns to offer good wishes.

HUNGARY
The groom gives the bride a bag of coins, while she gives him either three or seven handkerchiefs.

IRAN
During the ceremony, a canopy of cloth is held over the heads of the bridal couple by happily married women. The same women later scatter sugar over their heads for luck, scraped from decorated sugar cones called *kalehghand*.

ITALY
A ribbon is tied across the front of the church door to symbolise the bonding of the couple. Sugared almonds, or confetti, are tossed at the bride and groom for luck and fertility.

MALAYSIA
The gifts that the groom gives to the bride are carried to her house in procession by children. Each wedding guest is given a decorated egg, a symbol of fertility.

MOROCCO
Five days before the wedding, the bride is painted with henna on hands and feet, and adorned with jewels. After the wedding, she circles her new home three times.

NORWAY
The bride wears silver jewellery and a gold crown edged with small silver discs, the ringing of which frightens off evil spirits. Two small fir trees are planted on either side of the door to the couple's house until they have their first child.

POLAND
Reception guests pin money to the bride's veil. To ensure luck she has to drink a glass of wine without spilling a drop.

PUERTO RICO
A doll is dressed in a replica bridal dress and placed at the top table at the reception or perched on top of the cake. Little favours called *capias* are attached to it. The bride and groom pin one of these to each of the guests.

ROMANIA
Guests toss sweets and nuts at the new couple to wish them prosperity.

RUSSIA
After the ceremony, the bride and groom race to stand on a white rug. It is believed that whoever stands on it first will be master of the household.

SPAIN
The groom gives thirteen coins to the bride, symbolizing his ability to support her. During the ceremony, she carries them in a special purse.

SWEDEN
The bride has a silver coin from her father in her left shoe, and a gold coin from her mother in her right.

SWITZERLAND
After the vows are taken, the matron of honour sets fire to the bridal wreath (which symbolises the bride's virginity) and it is lucky if it burns quickly. A pine tree, symbolising longevity and fertility, is planted at the couple's home.

THAILAND
An older couple prepare the bridal bed with fertility symbols such as rice, sesame seeds, coins and a cat.

UKRAINE
A mock capture of the bride is carried out at wedding.

VIETNAM
The mother of a Vietnamese groom visits the bride's home on the wedding day to deliver betel and pink chalk (to symbolise a rosy future).

YEMEN
The wedding feast is prepared by the bride's relatives and includes small sweet fritters, which symbolise a sweet life for the newlyweds. It is the duty of all the guests to play music and sing for the bride and groom.

Chapter 8
HANDFASTING CUSTOMS

There are many customs and superstitions associated with weddings. In the past a wedding was seen as a time when people were particularly susceptible to bad luck and evil spirits. Many originated or are modifications of customs which began many centuries ago. They are maintained in the belief that they will bring good luck and happiness to the couple at a time when their lives are changing, hopefully for the better

TYING THE KNOT
"Tying the knot" and "getting hitched", "joining hands in marriage" are common terms for getting married. They originate in handfasting custom of trying the couple's hands together. Some covens just tie the right hands together. A more modern custom is to tie right hand to right hand and left hand to left hand to make an infinity symbol (like a figure eight). It is considered that as the hands are bound together, so the couple are joined in love, trust and mutual support.

Some covens allow the knots to be untied after the ceremony, while others insist that the couple remain bound for twenty four hours so that they realise the serious nature of the commitment, and just what is entailed in doing everything together. Don't worry, it can be great fun!

JUMPING THE BROOM
When I was a child, people who lived together without being married were spoken of as "living over the brush". This referred to an old custom that meant a man and woman who wanted to live together could jump together over a broomstick, and then be considered as common-law husband and wife. The old people maintained that this was a frequent practice amongst the Irish navvies (or 'navigators') that came to England to help dig the canal networks and build the roads.

The broom, or besom, was associated with the marriage rite in Britain for hundreds of years. One English custom was that, at the reception, the groom would hold the broomstick parallel to the floor, and all the young men would rush across the room in an attempt to be the first to grasp the handle; he would be the next to marry.

European gypsies also jumped the broom as part of the marriage ceremony. African slaves in America adopted the custom when they had the right to marry taken away from them. The custom still features in some African-American weddings as a recognition of their heritage. German immigrant brides were thrown over the broom by unmarried girls in Pennsylvania.

The broom is a symbol of fertility, with the handle representing the male (an obvious phallic symbol) and the brush the female, a suitable emblem of a union between a man and a woman. The handle is usually made from a male wood, and the brush from a female tree or shrub. . It is used to sweep the circle in an act of ritual purification and stands for the security of the hearth and home. It is an old fertility symbol, and in days past the women would ride them around the fields, leaping as high as they could on them; the higher they leapt, the higher the crops would grow.

Traditionally, the witches' besom is made of an ash stake with birch twigs and an osier (willow) binding. The birch is for the expulsion of evil spirits, the ash for protection and rebirth, and the willow in homage to the Moon Goddess. However, there are other alternatives that you might prefer:

ALDER   Support, foundation, magical beginnings, fire and water magic. A male wood used for the pole.

APPLE   An apple wand is used for love magic, for rituals designed to establish contact with the Otherworld, initiation, and for fertility rituals. A female wood-use the twigs for the brush.

ASH   The ash is a great conductor of magical force, traditionally used for witches' broomsticks, druids' wands and cunning men's staffs. The use of the ash wand connects the magician to all the three realms, and when using an ash wand he or she acts within all three. A male wood.

ASPEN   The aspen is used to invoke magical shields, for protection, and for healing. A male wood used for the pole.

BIRCH   The birch is a tree of fertility, but also a powerful magical force in rituals of purification and the banishment of negativity. A female wood used for the brush.

ELDER   Rites of the crone goddess, rites of Samhain and winter, fairy contact, healing, and summoning spirits. A female wood used for the brush.

ELM   Rites of the Goddess, feminine magic. Use for the brush.

HAWTHORN   Protection, invoking a psychic shield, fairy contact, the rite of Beltane and Goddess magic.

HAZEL   A good general-purpose wand, some say the most efficacious of all wands. A hazel wand is sometimes called the wishing rod. A male wood used for the pole.

HOLLY   Rites of male magic, warrior magic, protection from negative forces. A male wood used for the pole.

IVY   Binding magic, protection from psychic attack. Use for the bindings.

LINDEN   Feminine power and rites of the Goddess. Use for the brush.

MAPLE   Handfastings, rituals of celebration. Use as you see fit.

OAK   Rites of protection, general purpose magic, Midsummer, divination, fairy contact, Otherworld magic. A male wood used for the pole.

ROWAN   Protection, divination. A female wood use the twigs for the brush.

SPINDLE TREE   Spinning and weaving magic, creating magic, Goddess magic. A female wood used for the brush.

WILLOW   Bardic magic, healing, Goddess magic, feminine magic, rebirth, purification. Use for binding the broom.

The handfast couple usually leap the broom after the ceremony. Two people hold the broom at a convenient height so that they can jump over it, hand in hand, taking a leap into the future. Sometimes they are told that they must leap over once for each child they wish to have, others simply leap it three times.

JUMPING THE CAULDRON

An alternative is to jump the cauldron. A cauldron is essentially a cooking pot, a vessel which transforms the raw ingredients of life into something new. There are many cauldrons in Celtic myth, owned by various gods and goddesses. Some mysteriously produce sustenance, some transform; some hold the fruits of the harvest or give life. In essence all these cauldrons represent the transformative womb of the Goddess, which may be the vault of the heavens or the underground earth, in which seeds germinate and growth, and return to in death to grow once more- the cycle of all life. The cauldron is a symbol of initiation, renewal, rebirth and plenty. It may contain water, fire, incense or flowers as the occasion demands. Leaping over the cauldron, like leaping over the broomstick, is a fertility rite.

It is nice to fill the cauldron with water and float suitable flowers and herbs on the surface:

APPLE
Apple blossom is associated with the Goddess of fertility, lust, love and marriage. When an apple is cut in half it reveals a pentacle, the symbol of the goddess and the planet Venus, ruler of love.

BASIL
Basil is called the 'Witch's Herb' and throughout the ages witches have employed it in various forms of magic- for healing and revitalising the body and in love spells.

DAISY (ENGLISH) *Bellis perennis*
The daisy is associated with purity, innocence and faithful love.

MARIGOLD *Calendula officinalis*
Marigold is a herb of healing and protection, love and divination.

MARJORAM *Origanum vulgare*
Marjoram is sacred to the Goddess of Love and may be used to invoke her in all her aspects.

MEADOWSWEET *Filipendula ulmaria / Spiraea ulmaria*
Meadowsweet is sacred to Aine, Blodeuwedd, Gwena and Venus. Use for love, marriage and handfasting, fertility and plenty.

MYRRH *Commiphora myrrha*
Myrrh is a herb of love, fertility, death, regeneration and rebirth. It is sacred to Adonis, Demeter, Freya, Hathor, Hecate, Hera, Isis, Juno, Marian, Mut, Aphrodite and Dionysus. Use at weddings and handfastings.

MYRTLE *Myrtus communis*

Myrtle is dedicated to the planet Venus and the Moon, and sacred to Aphrodite, Artemis, Astarte, Ashtoreth, Freya, Hathor, Marian, Venus, Aphrodite, Myrrha, Thetis, The Graces and Hera. It is a tree which reflects the Goddess in all her aspects, and is employed for prophecy, love, fertility and marriage.

PRIMROSE *Primula vulgaris*

The primrose attracts love and glamour, and is sacred to Freya, Blodeuwedd, and all goddesses of the spring and love.

ROSE

Red roses are ruled by Jupiter, damask roses by the planet Venus and white roses by the Moon. The white rose represents purity, perfection, innocence, virginity and the Maiden Goddess, while the red is earthly passion and fertility, the Mother Goddess. Use rose petals for spells and rituals of love, passion, sexuality and sensuality, seduction and marriage, the Great Rite and handfasting.

ROSEMARY

Use also for healing, love, marriage, to keep a lover faithful, and for love spells.

VIOLET (SWEET)

Violet is a symbol of fertility, and frequently added to love potions. Mix with lavender to attract a new love. Violet is a symbol of the constancy of love and fertility. They are sacred to Aphrodite, Venus and other goddesses of love.

SHARING A CUP

The couple may wish to share a cup of wine as part of the formal procedure. Special loving cups with two handles are employed in some countries, or the cup can be a simple goblet or glass. Drinking from the same cup is a token that the couple will share everything from then on. Sometimes it is broken afterwards, as a sign that no one else shall share what they have.

THROWING THE BOUQUET

Throwing the bouquet may be a very old practice dating back to Pagan times. The bride tosses it over her head to the unmarried women who cluster behind her. The one who catches it will be the next to marry.

SHOWERING WITH RICE AND CONFETTI

In ages past it was the convention to shower the bride and groom with rice, grains, nuts, flower petals and sweets, partly as a an act of sympathetic magic so they would never go hungry, and partly as an invocation of fertility, represented by these items. Unmarried women often scrambled to pick up the grains so that the luck would rub off and they too would find a mate.

Today paper confetti is often used, but originally Italian confetti were sweets that were showered on the happy couple to indicate that their life would be sweet. In some places, the wedding cake was not eaten, but thrown at the bride!

Be wary of using rice which can be hazardous for any birds that eat it. Flower petals are a nice alternative, but can become slippery if too many are used. (The Victorians introduced the idea of a flower girl who strews the path of the bride and groom with blossoms.) If you use paper confetti, make sure it is environmentally friendly, and avoid the kind with non-biodegradable foil shapes or bleach and artificial colours .

SHOES

Shoes play a part in weddings in many parts of the world. We are familiar with the tying of old shoes on the back of the wedding car for good fortune, but in the Tudor period, the shoes would actually have been thrown at the bride and groom, and the luck was transferred if they were actually hit!

Another ancient custom, practiced by both the ancient Egyptians and Anglo-Saxons, was the passing over of a pair of the bride's slippers by her father to the groom, to symbolise the passing of authority from one to the other. The groom then tapped her on the head with one to indicate his dominance. Imagine a modern woman putting up with that!

Rather than throwing her bouquet over her shoulder, the German bride threw a slipper. Whoever caught it would be the next to marry.

THE HONEYMOON

The idea of the honeymoon comes from the ancient Teutonic people. The bride and groom kept their own company and drank honey wine for a full month, or moon, after the wedding, so this became known as the honeymoon period. Honey was widely believed to be an aphrodisiac in ancient and Mediaeval times and was an indispensable ingredient of love potions and spells or was taken with food and wine. Nowadays, the honeymoon is a special holiday away from everything for the newly married couple.

THE CAKE

The wedding cake probably originated with the ancient Romans, who baked small wheat or barley cakes and broke them over the bride's head as an act of fertility magic. Around 100 BCE they began creating small, sweet cakes that were eaten while the ritual was conducted. The custom seems to have spread throughout Europe in the following centuries. In the Middle Ages in Britain, small flat cakes containing fruit and nuts were piled up into a mound, the taller the better, and the bride and groom had to kiss over the top of it for good luck. After the wedding any leftovers were distributed among the poor. It was during the reign of Charles II of England that the cake was first iced when a visiting French chef decided to improve on the cake mound custom. Today's usual three tier wedding cake is said to be an imitation of the unusual spire of Saint Bride's Church in London. Such a cake was first baked for the wedding of Queen Victoria's daughter in 1859. It wasn't until the marriage of Price Leopold in 1882 that the supporting pillars were added.

The bride and groom make the first cut together as yet another mark that they will share everything. Every guest is given a slice, and those relatives and friends who are unable to attend the reception are sent a piece for good fortune. The top tier of the cake is often kept by couples for the christening of their first child.

A number of spells used to be performed with wedding cake, such as an unmarried woman sleeping with a piece under her pillow to dream of her future husband:

But madam, as a present take
This little paper of bride-cake;
Fast any Friday in the year,
When Venus mounts the starry sphere,
Thrust this at night in pillowbeer:
In morning slumber you will seem
T' enjoy your lover in a dream.

In Yorkshire a plate holding wedding cake was thrown out of the window as the bride returned to her parental home after the wedding. If the plate broke she would enjoy a happy future with her husband but if the plate remained intact her prospect would be grim. Another old English custom was to place a ring in the wedding cake. The guest who found it in their piece of cake would be ensured happiness for the next year. In the 1700's it became the tradition to thread a small piece of the cake through the wedding ring a certain number of times (nine being the usual number), and sleep with it beneath the pillow.

As a Pagan you might consider the relevance of the number three and the three tiers of the cake. It is a sacred number of the Goddess and refers to her triple aspects as Maiden, Mother and Crone. You can choose the colours of the icing and any decorations to reflect your personal beliefs and needs.

BRIDE ALE
In medieval England the tradition broadened to include the practice of washing down the cakes with a special ale called *bryd ealu* or "bride's ale," words that eventually became the word "bridal." See the recipes section.

FLOWERS
Flowers have played a part in weddings since the earliest times. They represent sweetness, beauty, joy and fecundity. They are employed today in the form of buttonholes, corsages, bouquets, posies, wreaths and table arrangements. For more information on flowers and handfastings, see the chapter on handfasting herb craft.

NUTS
Nuts are an obvious fertility symbol. They were once thrown at the bridal couple in place of rice or confetti. Guest favours often take the form of almonds.

UNITY CANDLE
This simple ritual is used by people of many different faiths as a symbol of joining. It utilises three candles. The outer two represent the bride and groom as individuals. They each lift their candle and use it to light the central, larger candle, as a symbol that what was once two has become one and cannot be separated. The side candles are then extinguished or left burning as you choose.

WISHING WELL
If the wedding takes place near a well, river or stream, the guests can thrown coins into the water invoking the water spirits to bless the couple.

EGGS
A natural symbol of fertility and promise, the egg features in many wedding customs. Sometimes they were thrown at the bride and groom (I presume they were hard boiled first) and sometimes painted and given to the couple or guests as gifts. In Ireland a laying hen was tied to the bed on the first honeymoon night in the hope that it would lay an egg which would be a fortuitous omen. Eating a double yolked egg was also thought to bring fecundity.

ROSES
The red rose is a symbol of love and passion, sacred to the Goddess of Love. You can present your beloved with a single red rose after taking your vows, as the first gift of your married life.

THE HEN NIGHT OR BRIDAL SHOWER

The hen night is held a night or two before the wedding for the bride and her friends to mark the last hours of being single. In Britain this takes the form of an evening out. In my own home town of Hinckley and in the surrounding villages the factory girls enacted an old custom that I have never seen elsewhere. During the lunch break on her last day as a single woman, the prospective bride was taken out and dressed in a hat made from paper flowers, and tied to a lamppost. The lamppost is probably just a more modern joke, but the flowered headdress may date back to old fertility customs. Pagan women may organise the evening a little differently, and spend the time making women's magic or telling women's stories over food and wine.

THE STAG NIGHT OR BACHELOR PARTY

While the women hold their hen night, the groom and his friends hold a stag party. In Europe, this term was once quite literal, when the man had to prove his virility by running with and hunting a stag. Ancient Spartan soldiers are thought to have been among the first to hold bachelor parties. The groom feasted with his comrades on the night before the wedding, swearing eternal friendship with them and saying farewell to his bachelor days.

Pagan men may go back to the roots of the tradition, and hold games and contests of skill, drink mead from the drinking horn and tell boastful stories of male prowess.

WEDDING FAVOURS

Pieces of the bride's attire were considered very lucky, and guests tried to steal pieces of it to take home. Desperate brides resorted to sewing ribbons onto their dresses, and this eventually evolved into the practive of giving wedding favours to the guests. In Italy they are given little bags of sweets, usually sugared almonds. Favours might include nosegays of herbs or flowers, packets of seeds or chocolates.

Chapter 9
WHAT TO WEAR

We have already discussed some clothing options in the section of themed weddings. This chapter contains some general advice on ritual clothing for handfastings.

Before you begin, take a minute or two to think about how you can make your wedding greener. Most wedding outfits are worn only once, even though a lot of materials and resources have gone into making them. Consider asking people to wear their favourite robes or outfits, or consider buying second hand clothes from online auctions or charity shops, and passing them on again after the ceremony.

THE WEDDING DRESS IN HISTORY

Bridal apparel has always been a matter of deep concern. What she wore might make good or bad magic for her subsequent life. We often associate the colour white with the wedding dress, but historically brides wore dresses of many different shades. Ancient Greek and Roman brides wore white to ward off evil spirits and to symbolise purity and innocence, but it was not often worn in Christian countries until the Middle Ages, when Anne of Brittany wore one at her wedding in 1499. There is not another mention of this until 1530 when the daughter of Henry VII, Margaret Tudor, married James IV of Scotland. Both bride and groom wore white damask edged and lined in crimson velvet. Until the Victorian era, girls usually just wore their best clothes until Queen Victoria made white fashionable by wearing it for her marriage to Prince Albert in 1840. However, there were various superstitions as to which colours were most suitable for a bride.

A Victorian verse states:

Married in Grey, you will go far away,
Married in Red, you will wish yourself dead,

Married in Green, ashamed to be seen,
Married in Blue, your love will be true,
Married in Pearl, you will live in a whirl,
Married in Yellow, ashamed of your fellow,
Married in Brown, you will live in a town,
Married in Pink, your spirit will sink,
Married in Black, you will wish yourself back.

Green was considered particularly bad as to say a girl had a green dress implied that she had been rolling about on the grass with a lover. In Ireland it was considered particularly unlucky as it was deemed the fairies' colour, and taboo for humans. The idea of the Irish bride in emerald green is a very modern one. In old China, the colour of love and luck is red, so is chosen for the bride's dress and the money envelopes that are presented to her. In Japan, white was always the colour of choice for bridal clothing, while Korean brides wear bright reds and yellows.

Other superstitions state that the bride should never make her own dress, that the final stitch should not be completed until she is departing for the ceremony, and that she should never try on the complete outfit before the day of the wedding, or mark the linen with her married name. This was thought to tempt fate by 'counting her chickens before they were hatched'.

COLOUR MAGIC
There is plenty of Pagan and magical lore about colours, and you might like to consider the following before designing your outfits:

WHITE is associated with the pale light of the moon and the fierce blaze of the sun. The Vestal Virgins wore white as a symbol of virtue. It symbolises light, purity, innocence, harmony, spirit, psychic development, the dispelling of negativity, purification, cleansing, tranquillity and protection

RED is a deeply linked with the supernatural. It is the colour of witchcraft; in fairy tales witches often wear red cloaks, have red hair or wear red caps. According to W. B. Yeats Irish witches put little red caps on their heads before flying off to the Sabbats. The Sussex witch Granny Smith was nicknamed Old Mother Redcap.

As the colour of blood, red is the colour of life, passion, lust and vitality, completion and harvest. Red represents influence and authority; red carpets are still unrolled for VIPs. It is a powerful colour, emblematic of fire, and as such is protective, effective against psychic attack.

GREEN is very much associated with fairies. They are often described as wearing green clothes, coats and caps. Some even have green skin. In Ireland green is so much the fairy colour that it is unlucky for humans to wear it, while in Scotland any woman dressed in green is sure to be a fairy.

Green is also described as the colour of envy. This may be because it is a colour of the Gods and spirits. Whatever the origin of the belief, the correspondence of green and envy has passed into folk custom. In Scotland it was the custom that if a girl married before her older sisters she should give them a present of green stockings, while in England an older sister should dance at her younger sister's wedding wearing green stockings.

Modern Pagans might wear green to symbolise fertility, prosperity, growth, creativity, love, change and balance

BLACK is the colour of darkness and night, linked with the planet Saturn, death and dissolution. Alternatively, it encompasses the rejection of ego, possibilities waiting to be realised, anticipation, strength, empowerment and wisdom. Witches often wear black robes.

BLUE is the colour of the sky, associated with the planet Jupiter and the bountiful Goddess. It is the colour of eternity, purity, faith, modesty, tranquillity, healing, spiritual development, protection and calm.

BROWN is the colour of earthiness, sexuality, practicality, the home and environmental awareness.

GOLD symbolises spiritual strength, spiritual zest, the sun, healing, wealth, divination, knowledge, the Sun God and service to others.

GREY connects with the planet Mercury and communication of all kinds.

INDIGO is the emblem of perceptiveness, vision, longevity and intuition.

MAGENTA is the colour of vision, creativity and insight.

ORANGE relates to optimism, success, courage, bravery and ambition.

PINK is the colour of love, friendship, happiness, harmony, peace, romance and compassion.

PURPLE represents strength, mastery and occult power.

SILVER is the colour of the moon, and the Moon Goddess, intuition, truth, enlightenment, poetry and inspiration.

TURQUOISE represents inventiveness, conception and philosophy.

VIOLET is the colour of   mastery, ceremony, spirituality, self-respect, spiritual growth and fulfilment.

YELLOW relates to the element of air, sound and speech, intellectual development and strength of mind.

THE VEIL

Ancient Greeks and Romans thought the veil protected the bride from evil spirits. Brides have worn veils ever since. The veil became popular in Britain in the eighteen hundreds as a symbol of modesty and chastity. In some Eastern countries where the marriage is arranged, the bride and groom do not see each other until after the ceremony is over and the veil is lifted from the bride's face.

THE GARTER

Western brides wear garters beneath their dresses. This may be thrown to the bachelors as the bouquet is thrown to the unmarried girls. The removal of the garter by the groom has a sexual connotation, and used to demonstrate the leaving behind of the virginal state.

THE HANDFAST CORD

Cords are very much associated with witches, who wear and keep cords for spell casting by knotting them in various ways. The use of knots in magic is very old, with their implications of tying and binding, untying and releasing. Some of the magical implications of knot magic still survive in the English language where people speak of marriage as 'tying the knot'. In some marriage customs of some parts of the world, the couple's hands are actually tied together to symbolise this, just as they are in the Wiccan ceremony of handfasting. When we part from someone, we may speak of 'severing the bond'. And, of course, the very first knot we all experience is the knot in the umbilical cord.

In ancient Egypt the knot was a symbol of Isis, usually depicted as a knotted cloth between her breasts. Ancient Romans were so in fear of the power of the knot to bind and limit energies, that the high priest, the *Flamen Dialis,* was forbidden to wear any knot or closed ring on his person, in case it bound up his powers.

The cords used to bind the couple's hands together in the handfasting ceremony should be made from a natural material such as cotton, wool or silk. You can plait different colours together to symbolise the weaving and joining of different forces and concepts. In length it should be some multiple of three 3 ft, 6 inches, 9 inches, 9 centimetres etc.

THE RINGS

Pagans often choose to exchange rings during the handfasting. Though it is not traditionally part of the service, it is customary in most parts of the modern world and a nice demonstration of commitment. The rings are placed on the Book of Shadows or the pentacle and blessed by the celebrant. The bride and groom then place them on each other's third finger of the left hand with words such as: *"This ring is the symbol of wholeness and perfection. It is a token of my love."* You might like to follow a medieval tradition and slip the ring onto three fingers in turn, saying *"In the name of the Maiden, in the name of the Mother and in the name of the Crone, I give you this ring in token of my love and commitment."*

The idea of the wedding ring dates back to ancient times, when a coin or ring would be split, with the bride receiving half, and the groom half, to demonstrate that they were two halves of one whole. When someone wears a wedding ring, it is an announcement to the world that they are married, part of a loving couple. It is a public symbol of a private commitment and a constant reminder of the pledges made on the handfasting or wedding day. There was an ancient Roman belief that a vein ran from the fourth finger of the left hand directly to the heart, and that placing a wedding ring on this finger insured the faithfulness of the heart. It used to be the case that when someone was divorced or widowed they took of their rings to show that they were single again.

For Pagans the ring also stands for the magic circle that guards the sacred rites of the Craft, and which stands for the wholeness of creation, and for the unified deity itself. The ring is a very ancient symbol of wholeness and perfection, a thing without beginning or end, of unity. Therefore the exchanging of rings is a magical act and a sacred oath before the Gods. All things in nature are cyclical—a circle is the symbol of the Sun, and the Earth, and the Universe. The whole circle symbolises continuity, eternity, completion and spacelessness: the absence of time and space. As it symbolises what is complete and unbroken, it also symbolises the Deity.

TYPES OF RING

While most people use plain gold bands as wedding rings, this was not always the case. Mary Queen of Scots sent a diamond ring to Thomas, Duke of Norfolk as a symbol of her willingness to marry him. Margaret Audley, the duchess of Norfolk, was shown with a large diamond on the third finger of her left hand.

Pagans are not limited to a single style of ring, and may chose something much more personal, perhaps using Goddess metals such as copper or silver instead of the usual gold. They may chose designs that have meaning for them such as pentacles, moons, gods and goddesses, hearts, ankhs and so on. I wear a silver ring with the three phases of the moon, with silver crescents of the waxing and waning moons set each side of a full moon made by a round moonstone.

THE SERPENT RING
Snake rings dotted with ruby eyes were popular wedding rings in Victorian England with the coils winding into a circle symbolized eternity. The serpent is a powerful Pagan symbol of regeneration, renewal and infinity.

CLASPED HANDS
A pair of gold rings was exchanged by Admiral Lord Nelson and his mistress, Lady Emma Hamilton, in the 17th century. They took the form of clasped hands, as a symbol of love. Nelson's ring is now kept at the National Maritime Museum at Greenwich in London.

THE CLADDAGH RING
This Irish design is used by many Celtic Pagans. It takes the form of a hand, a heart and a crown, signifying faith, love and loyalty.

THE POESY RING
The ring consists of from three to eight interlocking bands, each bearing a line of verse or word which creates a poem or motto. Some versions open to reveal a little heart. For example:

How do I love thee?
Let me count the ways
I love thee to the depth
And breadth and height
For the ends of Being
And ideal Grace [15]

THE PUZZLE RING
These consist of interlocking pieces that fall apart when the ring is taken off. According to one story, it was invented by a Sultan who wished to assure himself

---

15   Elizabeth Barrett Browning

of his wife's constancy. He knew that she would remove her wedding ring if ever she committed adultery and would not be able to reassemble it.

INSCRIPTIONS ON THE RINGS
A nice old custom is to have the rings engraved, usually in French or Latin. For example:

- *Nemo nisi Mors* (Till Death Divide)
- True Love
- Forever
- *Deux Corps une Coeur* (Two Bodies One Heart)
- With everlasting Love
- I am yours
- *Semper Amenus* (May we Love Forever)
- Love me truly
- *Tout pour bien Feyre* (In Good Faith)
- After consent, ever content
- Love me and leave me not
- In perfect love and perfect trust
- *Amor vincit Om* (Love Conquers All)
- *Mon Coeur Avez* (You Have my Heart)

USING GEMSTONES IN THE RINGS
Mining gold and gemstones uses a lot of energy and water, and can damage the environment. Your choices can make a difference. Choosing a vintage ring avoids using new materials. You can also buy rings made from recycled materials. Some companies can even make rings by melting down your unwanted jewellery. Choosing Fairtrade gold and silver means supporting companies who treat their workers fairly. You can also choose diamonds that haven't contributed to conflict in the place they were mined.

If your rings are to be set with gemstones, it is worthwhile making sure these are suitable for the purpose. Below is a table of gemstones and how they relate to love and marriage:

AGATE – It attracts good friends. Agate is particularly good for Geminis, but should not be worn by Pisceans or Virgos.

ALEXANDRITE – ensures luck in love

AMAZONITE – Increases courage and improves a woman's success in love.

AMBER – not a stone but a translucent fossil tree resin formed millions of years ago. It is pale yellow or brownish in colour, often with plants and insects trapped within.. The Norse believed that amber was the tears of the love goddess Freya, shed into the sea when her husband Odur (the summer sun) left her in the winter. It is particularly good for Leos.

AMETHYST (from Green *amethystos,* meaning "not intoxicating") – If a man wears it, good women will love him. Good for Pisceans. Brings luck and ensures constancy.

APACHE TEAR DROP – They are lucky and it is said that those who possess one of the stones will never have to shed tears again.

AQUAMARINE – represents marital harmony and is said to promote a long and happy marriage. Helps to attract a soul mate. Ensures constancy in a new bride.

AVENTURINE – brings luck in love.

BERYL – brings about love and harmony between married couples.

BLUE QUARTZ – may be worn by a man to attract a soul mate.

CARNELIAN (also Cornelian) – Helps both men and women attract a soul mate. Increases sexual desire.

CHALCEDONY – He who wears it will be lucky in law and love, energetic, strong, and free of melancholy, illusion and evil spirits.

CHRYSOPRASE – Should not be worn by Virgos or Pisceans. Improves a man's success in love and enhances success. Chrysophase enhances luck in love and helps mend a broken heart.

CITRINE – It is especially good for Geminis and increases feelings of self worth and confidence, especially for women. It can be used to infuse new life into a relationship that has gone stale.

CORAL – a stone, usually yellowish red or pink, made from the skeleton secreted by certain marine animals, and not a true gemstone. Helps you think and behave in a loving manner.

DIAMOND – set in gold and silver, diamonds became a popular choice for wedding and engagement rings from the fifteenth century. The Venetians believed that the diamond was created from the flames of love. The diamond is a talisman for reconciling husbands and wives who have quarrelled. It intensifies the properties of gems it is set with, particularly amethyst and emeralds. It is a symbol of eternal love.

EMERALD – Helps revive a stale romantic relationship.

GARNET – Give to a Leo to secure their love.

HAEMATITE – Increases self confidence and self esteem.

JACINTH – Deep yellow jacinth is taken in a potion to drive away melancholy and given to someone else to win his affection. They are good for Aquarians.

JADE (also Jadeite or Nephrite) – Give to an Aquarian to secure their love. Jade butterflies symbolise love at Chinese weddings.

KUNZITE – attracts love, often used in love magic.

KYANITE – attracts love. Give to a Taurus or Aries to secure their love.

LEPIDIOTE – improves openness and trust.

LOADSTONE (or Lodestone) – in mediaeval times used as a test for truth or faithfulness: "Lay this stone under the head of a wife. If she be chaste, she will embrace her husband. If she be not chaste, she will fall forth of her bed. Worn as an amulet the loadstone reconciles lovers' quarrels. They should never be used by Leos and Aquarians. Increases sexual desire and virility

MALACHITE – contains a great deal of copper (sacred to the goddess of love, Venus) which makes it green. Helps both men and women attract a soul mate.

MOONSTONE – is receptive, helps balance and soothe emotions, helps the higher self control emotions. Helps a woman attract a soul mate. If a man gives his woman a moonstone it will ensure her continued interest. Sacred to Venus the goddess of love, and often used as a love amulet.

OPAL – sacred to Venus, Roman goddess of love. It is said that if an opal wearer deceives another in love, or abuses a lover, the stone will bring them bad luck.

PEARL – the pearl is considered unlucky in a wedding or engagement ring as the shape looks like a tear, and thus the pearl is thought to bring tears. The exception is for those born under the sign of cancer. Give a pearl to a Cancerian to secure their love.

PINK CALCITE Helps foster feelings of love.

QUARTZ – Enhances the properties of other gemstones.

RHODONITE – attracts love.

ROSE QUARTZ – brings sleep, calms the emotions, eases the heart of traumas and leaves it open to love. Replaces resentment with inner peace. Often used in love spells. Helps dissolve all that burdens the heart. Promotes vibrations of universal love, knowledge of how to love and nurture the self and enlivens the imagination. Rose quartz channels love energy and improves a woman's success in love.

RUBY – excites sexuality, invigorates the root chakra, strengthens a good relationship and splits apart a bad one. Good for Capricorns, but should be avoided by Aries and Librans. Helps foster feelings of love and passion.

RUBY ZOISITE – increases sexual desire.

SAPPHIRE – set in a wedding ring, sapphire is said to bring marital happiness. You should not buy a sapphire for yourself, but it should always be a gift. If a man gives his woman a sapphire it will ensure her continued interest in him.

SMOKEY QUARTZ – improves a man's success in love and increases courage.

SPINAL – promotes sexual energy and desire. Good for Capricorns.

SUNSTONE – improves luck in love.

TOURMALINE – possesses both positive and negative poles electrically. These stones come in many colours from black, through green, pink, yellow, blue, white and red. A rare variety contains three colours in its make up. Attracts favours and friendship. Dark pink tourmaline improves a man's success in love. All colours channel love energy; give a watermelon tourmaline to a Gemini or Virgo to secure their love, a dark pink tourmaline to a Scorpio or Sagittarius, green tourmaline to a Capricorn, light pink tourmaline to a Libra. The red variety generally brings love.

TURQUOISE – blue brings together a man and wife who have quarrelled. Known as the stone of Venus and good for Taureans. The qualities are enhanced by being set in silver. Helps foster feelings of love.

UNIKITE – awakens love in the heart chakra, heals hurts to the emotions. Helps balance the emotions.

YELLOW ZIRCON – attracts love into your life.

Chapter 10
HANDFASTING HERB CRAFT

Using flowers and herbs at weddings is a very ancient custom. There are many ways to use flowers and herbs at a handfasting:

- In the incense
- As confetti
- Circle decorations
- Room decorations
- Altar decorations
- The bridal bouquet
- The maid's bouquets
- In baskets of flowers to be carried or for decoration
- In wreaths and chaplets for bride, groom, maids and groomsmen, and even for all the guests if you wish.
- Buttonholes for the guests
- Nosegays or posies for the guests
- For strewing
- In food and drink, including the Lovers' Cup
- In potions and spells
- In consecration oils and decoctions

THE VICTORIAN LANGUAGE OF THE FLOWERS
The Victorians popularised the use of flower symbolism for sending messages in the formalised Language of the Flowers. For example, if a man wanted to tell a woman that he loved only for her, he would send her a cedar leaf. Is she wasn't interested she might respond with burdock meaning 'touch me not' or, if his feeling were returned, with shepherd's purse meaning 'I give thee my all'. The practice was extended to use in the bridal bouquet, in which carefully chosen flowers might express constancy (bluebell), true love , fidelity (ivy) and so on. The first real floral "dictionary" was published in 1818, but others followed

and some disagreed on meanings, which meant that the giver and receiver were sometimes at cross purposes!

Acacia: friendship, chaste love
Acanthus: artifice
Achillea millefolia: war
Adonis: bitter memories
Agnus castus: coldness, indifference
Agrimony: gratitude
Allspice: compassion
Almond: hope
Aloe: sorrow, dejection
Althea: consumed by love
Alyssum, sweet: worth beyond beauty
Amaranth: unfading love
Amaryllis: splendid beauty
Anemone (garden): forsaken
Anemone (wild): anticipation
Angelica: inspiration
Apple blossom: preference
Arbour vitae: unchanging friendship
Arbutus: thee only do I love
Arum (cuckoo pint): ardour
Ash: grandeur
Aspen: lamentation
Asphodel: remembered beyond the grave
Aster: variety
Auricular, red: avarice
Autumn crocus: do not abuse me
Azalea: romance
Balm of gilead: relief
Balm: sympathy
Balsam: impatience
Barberry: sourness of temper
Basil: give me your good wishes
Bay: I will not change till death
Bee orchid: error
Beech: lover's tryst
Belladonna: silence
Betony: surprise

Bilberry: treachery
Bindweed: hopes extinguished
Birch: meekness
Birdsfoot trefoil: revenge
Bittersweet: truth
Black bryony: be my support
Blackthorn: difficulties
Bluebell: constancy
Borage: bluntness
Box: constancy
Bramble: remorse
Broom: neatness
Buckbean: calm repose
Bugloss: falsehood
Burdock: touch me not
Buttercup: childishness
Cabbage: profit
Cactus: thou leavest me
Calla lily: feminine beauty
Camellia, red: unpretending excellence
Camellia, white: perfected loveliness
Camomile: energy in adversity
Candytuft: indifference
Canterbury bell: gratitude
Carnation, striped: refusal
Carnation, deep red: alas for my heart!
Carnation, pink: woman's love
Carnation, yellow: disdain
Carnation: pure and deep love
Cedar leaf: I live for thee
Cedar of Lebanon: incorruptible
Celandine, lesser: joys to come
Centaury: delicacy
Cereus, night blooming: transient beauty
Cherry blossom: spiritual beauty
Chickweed: rendezvous
Christmas rose: relieve my anxiety
Chrysanthemum, yellow: slighted love
Chrysanthemum, red: I love
Chrysanthemum, white: truth

92

Cinnamon: forgiveness
Clover, four-leaved: be mine
Clover, red: industry
Clover, white: I promise
Cloves: dignity
Cockle: vain beauty is without merit
Colchicum: my best days have fled
Columbine: desertion
Convolvulus: bonds
Corcopsis: love at first sight
Coreopsis: always cheerful
Coriander: hidden
Cowslip: pensiveness
Cranberry: cure for heartache
Cress: stability
Crocus: cheerfulness
Crowfoot: ingratitude
Cucumber: criticism
Currents: thy frown will kill me
Cyclamen: diffidence
Cypress: despair
Daffodil: regard, chivalry
Dahlia: forever thine
Daisy, English: innocence
Daisy, garden: I share your feelings
Daisy, Michaelmas: farewell
Daisy, ox eye: patience
Dandelion: coquetry
Datura: deceitful charms
Dead leaves: sadness
Dittany of Crete: birth
Dock: patience
Dogbane: deceit
Eglantine: I wound to heal
Elder: compassion
Elecampane: tears
Elm: dignity
Endive: frugality
Eupatorium: delay
Evening primrose: inconstancy

Fennel: strength
Fern: fascination
Fig: argument
Filbert: reconciliation
Fir: elevation
Flax: I feel your kindness
Fleur-de-lis: I burn for thee
Forget-me-not: do not forget me
Foxglove: insincerity
Fritillary (crown imperial): pride of birth
Fritillary(snakeshead): persecution
Fuchsia : humble love
Furze: anger
Gardenia: ecstasy
Gentian: intrinsic worth
Geranium, ivy: bridal favour
Gillyflower: bonds of affection
Gladiolus: ready armed
Goat's rue: reason
Golden rod: encouragement
Gooseberry: anticipation
Goosefoot: goodness
Grape: charity
Grass: submission
Guelder rose: winter
Harebell: grief
Hawthorn: hope
Hazel: reconciliation
Heartsease: you occupy my thoughts
Helenium: tears
Heliotrope: devotion, faithfulness
Hellebore: scandal
Hemlock: you will be my death
Hibiscus: delicate beauty
Holly: am I forgotten?
Hollyhock: fruitfulness
Honeysuckle: the bond of love
Hop: injustice
Hornbeam: ornament
Horse chestnut: luxury

Hortensia: you are cold
House leek: domestic economy
Hyacinth: jealousy
Hydrangea: heartlessness
Hyssop: cleanliness
Ice plant: your looks freeze me
Ipomaca: I attach myself to you
Iris: message for you
Ivy: fidelity, marriage
Jacob's ladder: come down
Jasmine, cape: transports of joy
Jasmine, Indian: I attach myself to you
Jasmine, white: amiability
Jasmine, yellow: grace and elegance
Jonquil: return my affection
Judas tree: betrayed
Juniper: perfect loveliness
Kings-cup: I wish I were rich
Laburnum: pensive beauty
Lady's slipper: capricious beauty
Larch: boldness
Larkspur: fickleness
Lavatera: sweet disposition
Lavender: distrust
Lemon blossoms: fidelity in love
Lettuce: cold hearted
Lichen: dejected
Lilac: first emotion of love
Lily of the valley: return of happiness
Lily, day: coquetry
Lily, white: purity, sweetness, modesty
Lily, yellow: falsehood
Lime or linden tree: conjugal love
Liverwort: confidence
Locust tree: affection beyond the grave
Loosestrife: pretension
Lotus: forgetful of the past
Love in a mist: you puzzle me
Love lies bleeding: hopeless, not heartless
Lucerne: life

Madder: calumny
Magnolia: love of nature
Maize: riches
Mallow: sweetness, kindness
Mandrake: horror
Maple: reserve
Marigold, African: vulgar minded
Marigold, French: jealousy
Marigold, garden: sacred affection
Marigold: cruelty
Marjoram: blushes
Marshmallow: beneficence
Meadowsweet: usefulness
Mignonette: moral and mental beauty
Milkweed: hope in misery
Mimosa: sensitivity
Mint: virtue
Mistletoe: I surmount all difficulties and obstacles
Mock orange: counterfeit
Monkshood: a foe is near
Motherwort: secret love
Mugwort: happiness
Mulberry, white: wisdom
Mulberry, black: I will not survive you
Mullein: good nature
Mushroom: suspicion
Mustard seed: indifference
Myrrh: gladness
Myrtle: love in absence
Narcissus: egotism
Nasturtium: splendour
Nettle: cruelty
Nightshade: dark thoughts
Oak: hospitality
Oleander: beware
Olive: peace
Orange blossom: bridal festivities
Orange: generosity
Palm: victory
Pansy: think of me

Parsley: banquet, festivity
Pea: an appointed meeting
Peach blossom: my heart is thine
Peach: your qualities, like your charms, are unequalled
Pear: affection
Pennyroyal: flee way
Peony: shame
Peppermint: warmth of feeling
Periwinkle: sweet memories
Phlox: our souls are united
Pimpernel: rendezvous
Pine: endurance
Pineapple: you are perfect
Pinks, double red: pure and ardent love
Pinks, single red: pure love
Plane tree: genius
Plum: keep your promises
Polyanthus: heart's mystery
Pomegranate: foolishness
Poplar, black: courage
Poplar, white: time
Poppy: consolation
Pumpkin: coarseness
Quince: temptation
Ragged robin: wit
Ranunculus: you are rich in attractions
Raspberry: ingratitude
Reeds, split: indiscretion
Reeds: music
Rhododendron: danger
Rock rose (cystus): surety
Rose garland: reward
Rose leaf: I never trouble
Rose, Austrian: thou art all that is lovely
Rose, bridal: happy love
Rose, burgundy: unconscious beauty
Rose, cabbage: ambassador of love
Rose, damask: bashful love
Rose, dog (wild): pleasure and pain
Rose, Japan: beauty is your only attraction

Rose, moss: voluptuous love
Rose, musk: charming
Rose, one open and two buds: secrecy
Rose, red and white together: unity
Rose, tea: always lovely
Rose, white, dried: loss of innocence
Rose, white: I am worthy of you
Rose, yellow: decrease of love
Rosebud, red: confession of love
Rosebud, white: too young to love, innocence
Rosemary: remembrance
Rowan: I watch over you
Rudbeckia: justice
Rue: disdain
Rush: docility
Saffron: beware of excess
Sage: esteem
Scabious: I have lost all
Scarlet lobelia: preferment
Scotch thistle: retaliation
Service tree: prudence
Shamrock: light heartedness
Shepherd's purse: I offer thee my all
Snapdragon: presumption
Snowdrop: consolation
Snowdrop: hope
Sorrel: parental affection
Southernwood: jesting
Speedwell: warm feelings
Spindle tree: thy image is engraved on my heart
St John 's wort: animosity
Stock: lasting beauty
Straw, broken: quarrel
Straw, whole: union
Strawberry: excellence
Sunflower: false riches
Sweet pea: departure, delicate pleasures
Sweet william: frivolity
Sycamore: curiosity
Tansy: I declare against thee

Tare: vice
Thistle: austerity
Thyme: activity
Traveller's joy: safety
Tuberose: dangerous pleasures
Tulip, red: declaration of love
Tulip, yellow: hopeless love
Tulip: variegated: beautiful eyes
Valerian: accommodating disposition
Verbena: sensibility
Veronica: female fidelity
Vervain: enchantment
Vine: drunkenness
Violet, blue: faithfulness
Violet, sweet: modesty
Wallflower: fidelity in adversity
Water lily: purity of the heart
Wheat: prosperity
Willow, common: forsaken
Willow, weeping: melancholy
Wolfsbane: misanthropy
Yarrow: cure for heartache
Yew: sadness
Zinnia: I mourn your absence

PLANT MAGIC

Some of the Victorian language of flowers was simply made up by its creators, while some way based on ancient plant lore. Below is genuine magical plant lore, with some ideas on how to use the plants:

Apple

Apple blossom is associated with the summer goddess of vital energy, fertility, lust, love and marriage, called by various names: in Welsh myth, she is the goddess Olwen, She of the White Track; in Greek, Aphrodite, and in Latin, Venus, but she has many other names around the world.

The apple appears in Norse mythology in connection with love and fertility. In England apples were often used in love divination. To discover whom she would marry a girl would peel an apple and throw the unbroken peel over her shoulder. If it formed a letter it was the initial of her future husband.

Apple bark, blossoms and pips can be used in incenses for the planet Venus, the element of water and to consecrate emeralds and amethysts or to invoke a wren totem. Apple wands are employed for love magic.

Apricot

Apricot oil is reputedly an aphrodisiac. It is used as massage oil or as base oil for mixing in essential oils. Unfortunately it does not smell of apricots. Apricots make good additions to the handfasting feast.

Artemisia

In the Middle East, the bitter herb artemisia is incorporated into bridal bouquets to ensure that marriages will survive bitterness as well as sweetness.

Basil

By a slight stretch of imagination the leaves of basil can be seen as being heart shaped, and in folk magic this associates basil with love. In Moldavia girls would give young men sprigs of basil as a charm to make them fall in love with them, while in Italy girls would wear basil in the hair or rub the fragrant leaves on the skin to attract love; Spanish prostitutes still wear basil oil to attract custom. A pot of basil on a lighted windowsill was a covert invitation for a lover to call. In Voodoo bush basil (*O. minimum*) is sacred Erzulie, the goddess of love who is rather generous with her sexual favours. It is also sacred to Krishna, Lakshmi and Vishnu.

Basil may be employed in love incenses, the oil in love and attraction oils, and the leaves in food at the handfasting feast (or seduction dinners!).

Caraway

Caraway seeds are often used at weddings, both in the cake and thrown by guests for good luck. Caraway is said to help the couple to remain faithful. You might like to put some in the cake and in ritual cup. The rings may be consecrated with caraway oil or incense.

Clove

Cloves attract the opposite sex, and increase warmth and passion. Use some cloves in the ritual cup, or warm spiced wine at the feast. Clove oil may be used in anointing and love oil. **WARNING**: Can irritate sensitive skin.

Coriander

In the Middle Ages coriander was considered to be an aphrodisiac. The seeds were put into the popular drink '*hippocras*' which was commonly drunk at Tudor weddings. Coriander is widely used in love charms and incenses, especially if the couple want their love to last beyond this life, as it is a herb of immortality. It can be included in the ritual cup for handfastings. It can also be used to anoint the candles used in love magic.

Cinnamon
In sexual or tantric magic, cinnamon oil is used to anoint the body and stimulates the male passion with sun energy. Cinnamon sticks or powder may be mixed with other herbs in the ritual cup shared between a couple engaged in such practices, or indeed in the handfasting cup.

Clary Sage
Clary sage is a relaxing aphrodisiac. Use the essential oil in magical oils designed to attract the opposite sex, for love and harmony, as well as for divination, prophecy and clairvoyance.   **WARNING** Causes drowsiness, so do not drive or operate machinery after use. Use only in small amounts and do not use at all during pregnancy.

Cumin
Cumin increases feelings of warmth and passion. Use some cumin seeds in the food or add to spiced wine.

Damiana
Damiana has a reputation as an aphrodisiac. Mexican women take damiana infusion an hour or so before the sexual act. It is believed by some to have a tonic effect on the sexual organs and the central nervous system.
        The tea can be used in tantric and other sexual magic. It may be shared by a couple performing the Great Rite. Its reputation as an aphrodisiac may come from the fact that the alkaloids have a testosterone-like action. It may be used to strengthen the male sexual system and alleviate nervous problems of a sexual origin.

Dill
Dill increases a woman's desire for a man. Use some dill seeds in the handfasting feast.

Frankincense
The ancient Egyptians used frankincense during their rituals. It is cleansing, will dissipate negative vibrations, bad atmospheres and evil influences. It may be used before and after rituals to cleanse the atmosphere, raise vibrations, and

concentrate the mind. It is ruled by the Sun, and is sacred to Adonis, Apollo, Bel, Demeter, Helios, Ra, Sun gods, Venus, Vishnu and Moon Goddesses.

Gardenia
Gardenia increases sexual attractiveness in both men and women. It is widely used in love spells, oils and incenses.

Ginger
Used in love spells, increases passion, lust and warmth. Add some to the incense, or put a pinch in the food or wine.

Hibiscus
Hibiscus attracts love and is widely used in love spells. Wear hibiscus flowers behind your ear, decorate the table with them, use in the bouquet and arrangements. Add some dried hibiscus petals to the incense. Drink hibiscus tea.

Ivy
The evergreen ivy is a symbol of that which is undying and eternal. The Greeks used ivy to crown victors and newlyweds, because of the unchanging nature of the leaves it was a symbol of constancy, and it was used to decorate the altars of Hymen.

Jasmine
The name derives from the Persian word 'jasemin'. Persians used jasmine oil to perfume the air at banquets. It is called 'the king of flowers' and aromatherapists classify the dark essential oil, which has a faintly animal scent, as male. In China jasmine is associated with the feminine, female sweetness, and symbolic of women. Hindus value the jasmine flowers very highly and they are strung in garlands and presented to honoured guests. In Borneo it is the custom of women to roll up jasmine blossoms in their oiled hair at night to attract lovers. It is reputedly an aphrodisiac used in love sachets and incenses. Wear jasmine perfume at your pulse points for a sexual charge.

Lavender
Prostitutes often wore lavender as it was believed to arouse sexual desires in men. Lavender posies were often given to newly married couples to bring luck for the future. Make some lavender ice cream for the feast.

Lemon
Use in oils for love, attraction and sexual rituals, including the Great Rite.

Lemon balm

Lemon balm has a happy reputation as a healing and refreshing plant. In Southern Europe it is called 'heart's delight' and 'the elixir of life'. Lemon balm is connected with love shared under the influence of the Goddess. The leaves can be soaked in wine and the cup shared to strengthen the bonds between a magical group. A cup can also be shared between lovers, employed in spells and rituals designed to attract love and money. **WARNING** Do not use the oil during pregnancy.

Lemon verbena

Carrying lemon verbena is said to make you more attractive to the opposite sex.

Lotus

The lotus is considered by Hindus to be emblematic of the yoni. In Tantra, the yoni is symbolised by a red lotus. You can use this subtle emblem in the ritual without shocking granny.

In Chinese lore, the lotus has both masculine and feminine attributes since it grows out of the yin lunar watery element into the yang, the light of the sun. It expresses spiritual unfolding with its roots in the mud, growing upwards through the dark waters into the light and air. It is sacred to Kwan Yin, goddess of mercy and compassion.

The lotus is also sacred to the Canaanite goddess Quetesh who was depicted standing on a lion holding the lotus flower in one hand and serpents in the other, and Astarte who is shown standing on a lion with serpents encircling her waist. She wears a crown and holds a lotus flower in each hand.

Mandarin

Mandarin oil is called the 'oil of joy'. It lifts the spirits, stimulates and makes you glad to be alive. It is ruled by the Sun and the element of fire.

Marigold

In Tudor England, brides carried marigolds dipped in rosewater and ate them afterward, since they were thought to be aphrodisiacs. The marigold means fidelity in the west. In the east it is the flower of longevity and 'the flower of ten thousand years' this being synonymous with the uncountable, the endless.

Marigolds also feature highly in the lore of Mexico. It is believed that they grew where the blood of the natives, killed by the invading Spanish, touched the ground. It was sacred to the goddess Xochiquetzal, a flower goddess and mother of the maize god, also goddess of the underworld, sexual love and craftsmen. Marigolds were laid on graves and were particularly sacred to her.

Marjoram

The Greeks believed that Aphrodite created marjoram as a symbol of happiness and its scent came from its touch. Both the Greeks and the Romans used oregano to make garlands to crown newly married couples. Marjoram was an ingredient of 14th century love potions. Marjoram is associated with the Goddess of Love and may be used in handfasting garlands and incenses, or to honour or invoke love goddesses such as Venus and Aphrodite. Marjoram may be used as a bathing herb, as an incense or tea. Dried marjoram can also be used as incense or tea to help clear and harmonise the heart chakra.

However, aromatherapists consider that the middle note oil distilled from flowering heads of the sweet marjoram is an anaphrodisiac- it puts off potential lovers!

Meadowsweet

Also known as Bridewort, Bride of the Meadow and Mead Wort, meadowsweet falls under the dominion of Venus. It was one of the three most sacred herbs of the Druids (the others were watermint and vervain). It is sometimes known as 'Queen of the Meadows' which was one of the titles of the Celtic Goddess Blodeuwedd (flower-face). Legend says that she was created from nine flowers by the sorcerers Math Mathonwy and Gwydion as a bride for Llew, who had been cursed by His mother Arianrhod to the effect that he should never have a mortal bride. It was also sacred to the Celtic goddess Aine and the 'Celtic Venus' Gwena.

The folk name of 'bridewort' became popular because it was often used in bridal garlands and posies for bridesmaids. It was also frequently strewn in the church, on the path to the church and in the home of the newlywed couple. It flowers from June through to September and these were the most popular months for marriages in Druidic times. The folk name of 'mead-wort' comes from the fact that it was used to flavour mead. Meadowsweet beer was an old country beverage.

Myrtle

In Greek lore myrtle was sacred to the goddess of love, Aphrodite. At Temnos, Aphrodite was worshipped in the shape of a growing myrtle tree. Her attendants, the Graces, wore myrtle chaplets. It was used to honour her and used in bridal wreaths. The Athenians ate the fresh berries. The Romans dedicated it to Venus and used it during wedding celebrations. On April 23rd they celebrated the festival of the *Binalia Priora*, in honour of Venus. Ovid said: *'offer her incense and pray for beauty and popular favour. Pray that you might be charming and witty. Give to the queen her own myrtle and the mint that she loves and bunches of rushes concealed in clusters of roses.'*

In Arabian folklore when Adam was banished from paradise he took with him a sprig of myrtle from the bower where he first declared his love for Eve.

Northern European brides wear myrtle as a bridal wreath, in honour of Freya, the love goddess. She married Odur, symbol of the summer sun. One day he went away and Freya was sad without him. Her tears fell into the sea and were transformed into amber. She set out to look for him and crossed many lands. Her tears fell and became the gold found in those places. In the sunny south, she found him beneath the flowering myrtle. They returned home, the flowers bloomed, the grass grew green and the birds sang as they passed.

In Austria the bride might wear a bridal wreath of myrtle over her veil, while in Britain she gives her maids pieces of myrtle from her bouquet to bring them luck in love; if the plant roots and blossoms, they will marry soon. It was also the custom to plant a sprig from the bridal bouquet by the cottage door and many myrtle bushes owe their existence to this. The plant was said to flourish for as long as the marriage.

Myrtle is the luckiest flower for window boxes, laying a mantle of domestic happiness over the household. Planted in the garden it is said to ensure that love and peace reside within the home. Myrtle can be used in incenses connected with love, or incenses dedicated to Venus or Aphrodite.

Myrtle can be used in handfasting rituals. It can be carried by the bride, added to the incense or used to decorate the altar.

Neroli

A base note oil distilled from the blossoms of bitter orange, neroli is very relaxing, an aphrodisiac used to attract the opposite sex.

Orange

In Greek myth, all fruit bearing trees are the province of Demeter, goddess of marriage. In a Greek Orthodox wedding, crowns of orange blossoms were made for both bride and groom, and orange flowers were embroidered on the bride's dress.

The fragile blossoms symbolize innocence and virginity, as well as fidelity, eternal love and fertility. Saracens brides carried sprigs of orange blossom, and the tradition was introduced into Europe during the Crusades, though not in England, as the climate is too cold to support orange trees, except in the very expensive glassed 'orangeries' that were once enjoyed by the aristocracy. The orange tree has a magical reputation because it produces buds, flowers and fruit at the same time.

Patchouli

A base note oil distilled from the dried leaves, patchouli oil is an aphrodisiac, it stimulates sensuality and sexuality, and is therefore used in love and attraction oils. The oil is also useful as a fixative in perfumes and incense. Small quantities are uplifting, whereas larger doses are sedative.

Rose

The generic name '*rosa*' comes from the Greek '*rodon*' meaning 'red' as the roses of the ancients were a deep crimson colour. Aphrodite, the goddess of love, first emerged from the sea at the island of Cyprus, and where she stepped to shore the sea foam fell to earth in the form of white roses. In one tale, red roses were created when she scratched herself on a white rose while pursuing her lover Adonis, and it became coloured by her blood. In another, it was Adonis's shed blood that caused red roses to bloom, when he was killed by a boar. The white rose represents purity and innocence, while the red stands for passion.

The rose has always been an emblem of love, sacred to all goddesses of love. Roses were considered to be an aphrodisiac. It is said that Cleopatra seduced Anthony whilst standing knee-deep in roses. In Britain rose petals were scattered at weddings to ensure a happy marriage. In alchemy the rose symbolises mystical or divine love. Red and white roses together signify the union of opposites, the blending of fire and water, red signifies the masculine, the king, white is feminine, the queen. This symbolism is echoed in the Tudor rose, a symbol of reconciliation employed after the ending of the Wars of the Roses (1485) when the white rose of the House of York and the red rose of Lancaster were joined.

The Romans used the petals of the rose as a garland at their banquets. The guests were sometimes showered with rose petals but at one banquet so many petals showered down from the ceiling that some of the guests were suffocated. Roman brides and bridegrooms were crowned with roses, as were images of Cupid, Venus and Bacchus. Roses were scattered at the feasts of Flora and Hymen, in the paths of victors and on prows of war vessels. May 23rd was the Roman rose festival, the *Rosalia*, in honour of the goddess, Flora.

The rose symbolises love and the sacred marriage of the God and Goddess. Rose petals can be added to the cup into which the athame is plunged in obvious symbolism. The invoking Priestess might wear a chaplet of roses. Petals can be scattered around the circle as a blessing. Roses speak to us of the divine love of the Lord and Lady, the fruits of which brings life to the earth.

Rose oil is a useful oil for women, treating impurities in the womb, irregular periods and depression. It is ruled by the planet Venus and the element of water, and is used for spells of love, attraction, marriage and sensuality. It brings about a calm, peaceful atmosphere and induces harmony.

Rosemary
The Greek and Romans believed that rosemary symbolised love and death. Traces of rosemary have been found in ancient Egyptian tombs. Rosemary is also considered to be a herb of love. In some places rosemary is a wedding herb, all guests being greeted with a branch of rosemary wrapped in gold and ribbons. Sometimes it was used as a garland for brides, even for queens. The wood was employed to make musical instruments used to accompany love songs. In the language of flowers rosemary is seen as the symbol of fidelity, love, remembrance and friendship. Sprinkle powdered rosemary under the marriage bed to keep a couple together.

Sandalwood
A base note oil steam distilled from small drips and raspings of the heartwood of the tree, sandalwood oil has aphrodisiac properties and is used in love and attraction oils, and those used during sex rituals, including the Great Rite. Sandalwood chips may be added to the incense.

Vervain
Some people believe that the name of this herb was derived from *Herba veneris*, a name given to the plant by the Romans because of its aphrodisiac qualities. The Romans held that vervain was sacred to Venus, the Goddess of love, whilst to the Greeks it was sacred to Aphrodite, the root being worn by her priests in their robes. The ancient Egyptians believed that vervain had been formed from the tears of Isis. For centuries vervain retained its reputation as a herb of love and was a prime ingredient of love potions. Vervain was one of the three most sacred herbs of the Druids

Violet
The Greeks saw the violet as being a symbol of fertility, sacred to Aphrodite who is attended by the Three Graces, who weave her robes and plait her crown of violets. When she steps onto the shore, flowers spring up beneath her feet. The Romans too believed the violet to be a symbol of love and both they and the Greeks drank violet wine. Violets are seen as a symbol of the constancy of love and fertility. Owing to this they were often carried in love sachets, sometimes mixed with lavender to attract a new love, and frequently added it to love potions. Violets are also sacred to the Goddess of Love and may be used in incenses, garlands and temple decorations to invoke and honour her.

Yarrow

One of yarrow's folk names 'seven year's love' refers to the fact that it was thought that the yarrow had the property of being able to keep couples loving and faithful for seven years when used as a charm in the wedding bouquet.

Ylang ylang

A base note oil, ylang ylang is a calming, relaxing oil which lifts the spirits and engenders feelings of peace and harmony. It can be used for sexual problems, as it has aphrodisiac qualities. Use in oils of love and attraction. It is ruled by Venus and the element of water.

THE BRIDAL WREATH

The bridal wreath of chaplet of flowers is another circular symbol of eternity and perfection, reinforcing the idea of love as part of the cycle of life. Choose you favourite flowers and flower symbolism. The wreath can be simply constructed as follow:

Thick florist's wire
Thin florist's wire
Green florist's tape
Flowers
Ribbons

Use the thick wire to make a circle fitting the bride's head, leave a little extra space to accommodate the flowers and tape. Bind the flowers to the circlet using the thinner wires and cover with the green tape. Bind the flowers close together and intersperse with greenery and gypsophillia for a really stunning look. Add coloured ribbons at the back.

Alternatively, you might purchase a bridal crown or tiara and cover this with flowers or herbs.

THE BOUQUET

It is possible that the Stone Age bride went to her nuptials carrying a posy of wild flowers, though it is unlikely that we will ever know for sure when the custom first began. Certainly it is very ancient and widespread. In ancient Rome, Greece and Egypt brides carried sheaths of wheat and grains. This developed into a lose bunch of flowers, and during the Middle Ages, English brides carried round posies or nosegays of sweet smelling flowers and herbs.

I feel it is much lovelier to make your own bouquet, preferably with wild flowers or flowers from your garden, or to have it made by a friend as an act of love, rather than just buying one from a professional florist. In the past the bouquet was usually made for the bride by her mother.

Different flowers have always been considered as having certain virtues and a magical significance, and this has already been discussed. An old English custom is to have love knots of ribbon hanging from the bouquet.

INCENSES

Loose incense is probably the easiest type of incense to make, and the most useful kind for magical ritual. The recipes in this book are all for loose incense.

First of all assemble your ingredients, your pestle and mortar, your mixing spoons and your jars and labels ready for the finished product. All the measurements in this book are by volume, not weight, and I use a spoon to measure out small quantities when I am making a single jar of incense, or a cup for large quantities and big batches. Therefore when the recipe says 3 parts frankincense, ½ part thyme and 1 part myrrh, this means three spoons of frankincense, half a spoon of thyme and 1 spoon of myrrh.

When using resins and essential oils, these should be combined together first, stirring lightly with the pestle and left to go a little sticky before you add any woods, barks and crushed berries. Next add any herbs and powders and lastly any flowers.

As you blend the incense concentrate on the purpose for which the incense will be used, and 'project' this into the blend. If you like you can make a whole ritual of the event, perhaps even picking and drying your own herbs, then laying out the tools and ingredients on the altar, lighting a candle and asking the God and Goddess for help: *"God and Goddess, deign to bless this incense which I would consecrate in your names. Let it obtain the necessary virtues for acts of love and beauty in your honour. Let Blessing Be".*

The incenses should then be stored in screw topped glass jars.

Burning Incenses

Loose incense is burned on individual self-igniting charcoal blocks, or thrown directly onto the bonfire. To use your incenses, take a self-igniting charcoal block (available from occult and church suppliers) and apply a match to it. It will begin to spark across its surface, and eventually to glow red. Place it on a flame-proof dish with a mat underneath (it will get very hot). When the charcoal block is glowing, sprinkle a pinch of the incense on top- a little goes a long way. Alternatively, if you are celebrating outdoors and have a bonfire, you can throw much larger quantities of incense directly onto the flames. I have also sprinkled it on the hot plate of my Rayburn, and this smoulders away quite nicely, though it would really mess up a gas or electric hob!

A useful tip is when a packet of charcoal blocks has been opened they will quickly start to absorb moisture from the air. This makes them difficult to ignite. Pop them in the oven for ten minutes on a low heat to dry them out, and they will light easily.

HANDFASTING INCENSE

3 parts frankincense
1 part copal
1 part red rose petals
Few drops rose oil
Few drops orange oil
½ part cinnamon powder
Method
Mix together and burn on charcoal.

LOVE INCENSE

½ part thyme
3 parts red sandalwood
1 part red rose petals
Few drops lavender oil
½ part lavender flowers
½ part basil leaves
Method
Mix together and burn on charcoal.

LOVE #2

½ part thyme
3 parts red sandalwood
1 part red rose petals
Few drops bergamot oil
Few drops lavender oil
½ part lavender flowers
½ part basil

TRUE LOVE

3 parts frankincense
Few drops patchouli oil
½ part orris root
½ part cinnamon root

EROS (Greek God of Love):
1 part red rose petals
½ part bay leaves
1 part dog rose petals
4 parts acacia resin

FREYA (Teutonic Moon/love Goddess):
½ part primrose flowers
½ part cowslip flowers
½ part cypress needles
1 part mistletoe twigs and leaves
½ part rose petals
½ part daisy petals
½ part strawberry leaves
½ part myrtle,
½ part red clover flowers
5 parts myrrh
2 parts benzoin,
3 parts red sandalwood
Few drops rose oil (optional)
Few drops sandalwood oil

HULDA (Teutonic Goddess of marriage and fertility):
1 part flax flowers
1 part rose petals
1 part dog rose hips
2 parts elder wood
½ part elder blossoms

APHRODITE (Greek Goddess of Love):
½ part cypress needles
A few drops cypress oil
3 parts benzoin
½ part rose petals
1 part apple wood
¼ part cinnamon sticks
¼ part daisy flowers
A few drops geranium oil
¼ part violet flowers

ASTARTE (Canaanite Fertility Goddess):
3 parts acacia
1 part myrtle blossoms
1 part pine wood
½ part pine resin
Few drops pine oil
2 parts sandalwood
1 part red rose petals
Few drops orange oil
1 part jasmine flowers
3 parts frankincense

APOLLO (Greek and Roman God of the Sun, Poetry and Medicine):
½ part bay laurel leaves
½ part peony flowers
2 parts aspen wood
2 parts frankincense
½ part cypress needles
½ part fennel seeds
2 parts acacia
Few drops bay oil

ADONIS (Greek Vegetation God):
½ part fir needles
1 part myrrh
½ part anemone flowers
2 parts frankincense
1 part acacia resin
Few drops bay oil
½ part narcissus flowers

BRIDE
1 part heather flowers
3 parts myrrh
½ part celandine
½ part angelica flowers
½ part basil

CERNUNNOS (Celtic Horned God):
½ part betony herb
1 part pine resin
Few drops pine oil
2 parts oak wood
½ part camomile flowers
½ part yarrow herb
1 part lavender flowers
1 part cedar wood
1 part ash wood
½ part bistort root
½ part nettle herb

CUPID (Roman God of Love):
1 part rose petals
Few drops rose oil
1 part cypress needles
½ part bay leaves
½ part briar rose hips

DEMETER (Greek Corn Goddess):
½ part grains of corn
1 part rose petals
2 parts frankincense
2 parts myrrh
½ part pennyroyal herb
½ part bean flowers
½ part red poppy petals
½ part cypress needles
Few drops rose oil (optional)
Few drops cypress oil

EROS (Greek God of Love):
1 part red rose petals
½ part bay leaves
½ part briar rose hips
Few drops rose oil
1 part frankincense
1 part myrrh

ERZULIE {Haitian Voodoo Goddess of Love):
1 part basil herb
2 parts crushed cardamom pods

HERA (Greek Queen of Heaven):
1 part apple blossom
2 parts willow
½ part iris petals
Few drops cypress oil
½ part red poppy petals
3 parts myrrh
1 part pear bark

JUNO (Roman Queen of Heaven):
3 parts myrrh
Few drops myrrh oil
½ part olive leaves
½ part iris petals
½ part orris root powder

MAGICAL OILS

Magical oils can be used in several ways:

1. In the bath – add two teaspoons of blended magical oil to the bath after it has run. Swirl it about in the water to ensure dispersion over the surface. As you get into the bath the oil will coat your skin, and the heat of the water helps its absorption. You will also breathe in the vapours. For an oil bath do not use soap – treat it as a ritual, not a wash. A purification bath is a pre-requisite to any ritual, and you can add an appropriate oil to help you attune to the ceremony to come.

2. Anointing – most magical groups anoint coveners as they enter the circle, during initiation rituals etc. Magical tools are anointed as part of their consecration.

3. Vaporisation – all essential oils readily evaporate and may be used in the place of incense if this is more convenient. Bear in mind that in this case they represent the element of fire, rather than air, within the circle. Purpose made oil evaporators should be used.

4. An oil may be used to 'seal' a doorway or window against negativity after a cleansing or exorcism has taken place. A suitable oil is smeared around the opening.

Do not take any of the oils internally. The oils are highly concentrated and can be damaging or even poisonous when taken internally.

TYPES OF OILS

There are two types of magical oils that I use. The first type I make from herbs and flowers that I collect or grow. It is impossible to make essential oils at home, so I make infused oils (see below). The second type I make are blended oils, made with a base oil and drops of bought in pure essential oils added.

Making Infused Oils

Loosely fill a clear glass jar with freshly picked sprigs of herbs or flowers. Fill the jar with a vegetable oil (almond or sunflower are best). Cover the top of the jar with a piece of muslin and leave on a sunny windowsill for about two weeks, stirring daily. Strain into a clean jar or bottle. This oil will keep for around 4-5 months in a cool, dark place. There is no need to dilute it any further for use, but you can blend together several varieties if you wish.

Making Blended Oils

The recipes in this book are for blended oils. They are formulated using 20 ml of base oil (see below) and the stated number of drops of essential oil. Essential oils are readily available. They are quite expensive, but a little goes a long way- you only use a few drops at a time. Try buying three or four 5 ml bottles to begin with, and you could gradually build up your collection. Undiluted essential oils, stored in a cool, dark environment, will last for several years. Essential oils are far too concentrated to use alone. They could cause serious damage if used undiluted. Always make sure that you buy *100% pure essential oils* from a reputable supplier. Perfume oils are synthetic and have no therapeutic or magical effect. If you wish the oil to keep for longer than a few weeks you will have to use a base of wheatgerm oil, or add 20-30 drops of pure vitamin E oil to the blend. I have oils that have kept for years based on this prescription.

Base Oils

Base oils, which make up the bulk of your formula, should be vegetable in origin- never use mineral oils, including baby oil. Suitable oils include avacado, hazelnut, wheatgerm, grapeseed, olive, sunflower, rapeseed, soya and almond. You will find most of them in the supermarket (yes – the same stuff you cook in!).

LORD AND LADY
Rose 10, cinnamon 4, myrrh 3, frankincense 3

LOVE
Bergamot 5, lavender 5, clove 1, cinnamon 1

LOVE DRAWING
Rose 15 lavender 5

ANOINTING
Myrrh 4, cinnamon 4

CLEOPATRA'S SEDUCTION OIL
Jasmine 5, myrrh 5, frankincense 3, rose 8

CONSECRATION
Clove 4, lemongrass 8, thyme 8
TEMPLE
Rosemary 3, frankincense 3, thyme 4

VENUS LOVE OIL
Verbena 2, lemon 5, orange 5

VENUS
Thyme 7, cedar 9, benzoin 4

MAKING MAGICAL BATH SALTS

Take 1oz or 28 gms of salt and place in a non porous ceramic basin and add a total of 6-8 drops of undiluted essential oil (see the section on magical oil recipes and adapt these to the required amount). Blend in with a pestle and place in an airtight jar until required. If you like, you can add colour in the form of food colouring as a further resonance of magic. This colour should be added before the oil and blended until it is smooth throughout. The bath salts may be used in the pre-ritual bath for cleansing the body and aura, and to help you attune to the matter in hand.

Chapter 11
THE HANDFASTING FEAST

Around the world there are many different traditional wedding foods. Here in Britain the wedding cake is a rich, iced cake, full of nuts and fruit that represent fertility and prosperity, since such ingredients were once very rare and expensive. The Icelandic wedding cake is called *kransakaka* and consists of rings of almond pastry of various sizes piled on top of one another, decorated with swirls of icing, while the hollow centre is filled with sweets and chocolate. The Dutch feast is characterised by a sweet called "bridal sugar" and spiced wine called "bride's tears". In the Mediterranean, breads take centre stage, and are often decorated with beads and flowers. The bride and groom are offered a cake made of honey, sesame seed and quince. Italian wedding banquets may include as many as fourteen courses, ending with a range of desserts such as sugar coated almonds, twists of fried sugared dough, heart-shaped biscuits and so on.

Greek weddings feature nuts, with sugar coated almonds, or *koufetta*, placed in odd numbers in little bags. The odd number signifies that they are undividable, and the couple must share them. The *koufetta* are also carried to guests on a silver tray; if an unmarried woman takes them off the tray and puts them under her pillow, she will dream of the man she'll marry. In some of the Greek islands, the wedding ceremony will end with honey and walnuts offered to the bride and groom from silver spoons. Walnuts easily break into four parts, standing for the bride, groom and their two families.

Chinese weddings are a demonstration of the generosity and wealth of the family with elaborate twelve course banquets which should have enough left over to feed the poor. Things are simpler in Korea, where a simple 'noodle feast' is served consisting of a single dish of long noodles which symbolise a long and happy life.

The hot spices, such as ginger, cinnamon, cumin, cardamom, anise and clove are said to promote sexual energy and passion. Anise was an ingredient of the Roman wedding cake, the forerunner of our own traditional iced fruit cake.

Caraway is said to help lovers remain faithful, while dill strengthens the bonds of a couple. Coriander is a herb of love and harmony and has been used in love charms for hundreds, if not thousands, of years. Cinnamon and yarrow stimulate male sexual energy.

Some ingredients honour the Goddess of Love and her gifts, such as meadowsweet, strawberry, saffron, apple, sorrel, mallow, violet, peppermint, catmint and red roses. Clove, basil, apricot, lemon, lime, vanilla and lemon balm attract love. Both rosemary and violet mark boundaries and rites of passage- the passage from the single state to the married one, the leaving behind of one life and the beginning of a new one as a couple. Marjoram helps to harmonise the heart chakra and promote unselfish love.

The period after the marriage is called 'the honeymoon' from the practice of the ancient Germans of drinking honey wine for thirty days after the marriage. Honey was widely believed to be an aphrodisiac in ancient and mediaeval times and was an indispensable ingredient of love potions and spells or was taken with food and wine.

SAVOURY DISHES

CHEESE AND HAZELNUT PATE
4 oz Lancashire cheese
4 oz hazelnuts
4 oz butter

Method
Blend all the ingredients together in a food processor, or grind with a pestle and mortar until smooth.

HAZELNUT TART
8 oz wholemeal pastry
1 onion
1 oz butter or margarine
3 oz ground hazels
2 eggs, beaten
¼ pt stock
1 tsp. Marmite (yeast extract)
1 tbs. fresh sage, chopped
Salt and pepper

Method
Line a flan dish with the pastry. Cook the finely chopped onion in the butter and

add the other ingredients. Pour into the pastry case and bake in a moderate oven at 350°F/180°C/gas mark 4 for 40 minutes.

NUT ROAST
1 onion
1 tbs. oil
1 oz flour
¼ pint stock
Mixed herbs to taste
½ tsp. Marmite
12 oz ground mixed nuts
4 oz brown breadcrumbs
1 oz rolled oats
4 tomatoes
4 oz mushrooms
2 eggs
Seasoning to taste

Method
Chop the onion and cook in the oil until soft. Add the flour and stock and stir to thicken. Add the herbs and marmite, simmer over a low heat for five minutes. Remove from the heat. Meanwhile, in a large bowl, mix the nuts, breadcrumbs, oats, tomatoes, mushrooms and seasoning. Add the beaten eggs and the cooled onion gravy. Mix thoroughly. Spoon into a greased 2lb loaf tin and bake for 30-40 minutes at 190°C/375°F/gas mark 5

COLL CAKES
6 oz ground hazel nuts
½ cup of honey
1 oz flour
1 tbs. grated lemon peel
1 beaten egg
1 tbs. lemon juice
Method
Blend the honey and ground nuts into a paste. Mix in the flour and lemon peel. Blend the lemon juice and egg together and add to the mixture. Drop small amounts onto a greased baking tray and bake at 180°C/350°F/gas mark 4 for 20 minutes.

BASIL AND LOVE-APPLE MOULD
1 lb. tomatoes

½ pt tomato puree
Tabasco
Worcestershire sauce
Handful basil, shredded
2 cloves garlic, crushed
Juice of ½ a lemon
Stale bread slices
1 tsp. sugar

Method

Scald tomatoes and remove skins. Chop roughly. Stir garlic, basil and sugar into tomatoes and season. Put the tomato puree in a shallow dish and stir in a little Tabasco sauce, Worcestershire sauce and lemon juice. Cut out one slice of bread to fit the base of a 1 pint pudding dish and dip it into the puree mixture, coating both sides. Place the coated bread in the bottom of the dish. Cut the other slices to fit around the inside of the dish, coating them in the puree mixture before pressing into place. Pour in the tomatoes, basil and garlic. Drizzle olive oil over the surface and top with more coated bread. Place a weighted plate on the top and put in the refrigerator overnight, remembering to put a plate underneath to catch any spillage. Turn out onto a plate and serve with salad.

HERB SALAD
½ lb. tomatoes, sliced
½ cucumber, sliced
1 red pepper, sliced
6 spring onions, chopped
½ lettuce, shredded
1 small sprig thyme, finely chopped
1 sprig marjoram finely chopped
2 tarragon leaves, finely chopped
¼ pt plain yoghurt

Method

Mix together the herbs and the yoghurt.
Arrange all the other ingredients in a salad dish and dress with the yoghurt mixture.

SWEET DISHES

HANDFASTING CAKE
5 oz plain flour
½ pint milk

1 tsp. baking powder
1 heaped tsp. caraway seeds
4 oz castor sugar
2 egg whites
2 oz candied peel
Pinch salt
3 oz butter

Method

Cream together the butter and sugar and stir in the milk. Whip the egg whites until stiff and gently fold into the mixture. Add the salt and baking powder and flour. Add the candied peel and caraway seeds. Pour into a greased and lined 8" round tin and bake in a moderate oven at 180°C/350°F/gas mark 4 for 80 minutes.

LEMON AND GINGER MUFFINS

1 lb. plain flour
1 level tsp. salt
1 oz fresh yeast
¼ pt cold milk
¼ pt boiling water
1 beaten egg
1 oz melted butter
Finely grated rind of 1 lemon
1 tsp. ground ginger

Method

Sift together the flour and salt. In a jug, mix together the milk and water, and stir a little into the yeast to make a cream. Pour this cream into the milk and water and stir well. Mix into the flour with the egg to form a soft dough. Turn out onto a floured board and knead until it is no longer sticky. Cover and leave in a warm place until it has doubled in size. Knead again on a floured board sprinkled with the lemon rind and ginger, so that they are incorporated into the dough. Roll out to ½" thick. Cut into rounds with a 3" cutter and arrange them on a well floured baking tray, allowing space between each. Dust the rounds with flour. Cover again and leave them to double in size. Bake at the top of the oven at 250C/450F/gas mark 8 for 5 minutes.

GINGER ROLL

1 packet ginger biscuits (cookies)
½ pt whipping cream
1 glass sherry

Fruit left over from a fresh fruit salad

Method

Whip the cream until very stiff. Dip a ginger in the sherry and immediately spread with whipped cream. Do the same with a second ginger and sandwich them together, plain side to creamed and stand them on edge to form the beginning of the log. If desired you can place a small piece of fruit in between each biscuit. Continue in this way with the remaining biscuits, until your log is of the desired length. Cover with the rest of the cream and chill thoroughly for at least half an hour. Decorate with more fruit and serve. The ginger will have softened and will melt deliciously in the mouth.

TUDOR FLAN

3 tbs. runny honey
¼ pt water
2 oranges, thinly sliced
8 oz shortcrust pastry
¼ pt whipped double cream
2 oz sugar

Method

Mix the honey and water. Drop in the orange slices and stand overnight. The next day, place this in a pan and simmer for 30 minutes. Line a flan dish with the pastry and bake blind at 220°C/425°F/gas mark 7 for 15 minutes in a hot oven. Leave to cool. Meanwhile drain the oranges from the syrup and leave to cool slightly. Spread the bottom of the pastry case with cream and arrange the orange slices on top. Add the sugar to the syrup, bring to the boil and simmer for 5 minutes until the liquid thickens. Spoon over the orange slices.

HONEYDEW CAKE

6 oz plain flour
½ level tsp. bicarbonate of soda
¼ level tsp. ground cloves
1 level tsp. cinnamon powder
3 oz demerara sugar
3 tbs. honey
2 tbs. golden syrup
1 egg, beaten
2 tsp. lemon juice
Pinch of saffron
to decorate:
1 oz softened butter

3 oz icing sugar

2 tbs. honey

Method

Set the oven to180°C/350°F/gas mark 4 . Put the saffron to soak in the lemon juice. Lightly oil a 7" cake tin, preferably a heart shaped one if you have one, and line the base with oiled grease proof paper. Sift the flour, soda, cinnamon and cloves into a bowl and make a well in the centre. Put the butter and sugar into a pan with the honey and syrup and melt over a low heat. Pour into the flour well, and mix with a wooden spoon. Add the beaten egg and saffron lemon juice, and continue beating until smooth. Pour into the tin and bake in the centre of the oven for 35-40 minutes. Leave to cool for 5 minutes and turn out onto a cooling rack. Remove the paper. To decorate beat together the butter, icing sugar and honey. Spread over the top of the cake and place in the fridge to set. This cake is best made a few days in advance as the flavour improves with keeping. Wrapped it will keep for around 14 days. The top can be decorated with crystallised ginger, crystallised violets, strawberries, or any seasonal, edible flowers or fruit.

BRIDAL CAKE

8oz butter

8oz sugar

3 tbs. honey

Rind 1 orange, grated

4 eggs

2 tbs. liqueur (whatever you like)

12 oz plain flour

1 level tsp. baking powder

Pinch salt

2 oz ground almonds

1 lb. 4 oz mixed dried fruit

4 oz chopped glace cherries

for the topping:

halved nuts and crystallised fruits

Method

Set the oven to 180°C/350°F/gas mark 4. Cream the butter and sugar. Beat in the honey and orange rind and add the eggs a little at a time. If the mixture curdles add a little flour. Add the liqueur. Fold in the flour, baking powder and salt, then the mixed fruit and cherries. Spoon into a well greased and lined tin and bake in the centre of the oven for 45 minutes then reduce the temperature to 170°C/325°F/gas mark 3 and continue to cook for around an hour and a half. Remove from the oven and cool in the tin for half an hour. The cake may be wrapped in grease proof paper and foil and stored in a tin until ready for use. To decorate, remove all the wrappings and glaze with apricot jam and arrange the fruit and nuts on top.

ROSEMARY FRUIT CAKE

6 oz butter
6 oz soft brown sugar
3 eggs, beaten
8 oz plain flour
1 tsp. baking powder
1 lb. mixed dried fruit
1 tbs. chopped fresh rosemary leaves

Method

Grease an 8" cake tin and line with grease proof paper. Cream the butter and sugar and gradually beat in the egg and add the flour, folding it in with the baking powder. Add the fruit and rosemary. Spoon into the tin. Cook at 170°C/325°F/ gas mark 3 for about one and a half hours. Reduce the temperature to 150°C/ 300°F/gas mark 2 and cook another hour. Cool in the tin.

GINGER CAKE

8 oz plain flour
4 oz butter
½ tsp. bicarbonate of soda
2 oz black treacle
2 oz golden syrup
4 oz brown sugar
1 egg
2 tbs. milk
1 tsp. ground ginger

Method

Cream the butter and sugar. Warm the treacle and syrup and add to the butter and sugar. Gradually add the beaten egg, flour and ginger. Dissolve the bicarbonate of soda in the milk and add to the mixture. Grease an 8 inch cake tin and spoon in the cake mix. Bake at 150°C/300°F/gas mark 2 for 60 minutes.

IRISH WHISKEY CAKE

2 ¼ lb. mixed dried sultanas, raisins and currants
2 oz mixed peel
2 oz glace cherries

2 oz chopped walnuts
¼ pint whisky
¼ pint milk
12 oz muscavado sugar
12 oz butter
4 eggs
1 lb. 4 oz plain flour
1 level tbs. baking powder
2 level tsp. mixed spice
to glaze:
2 tbs. apricot jam

Method

Place the dried fruit and peel in a bowl. Stir in the whisky and milk, cover and leave overnight. Heat the oven to 140°C/275°F/gas mark 1. Oil a large tin (approx. 12inch x 10inch) and line the base and sides with grease proof paper. Brush the paper with oil. Cream the butter and sugar, add the beaten eggs a little at a time. If the mixture curdles add a little flour. Sift the flour, baking powder and spice and fold into to the creamed mixture. Add the fruit, nuts and whisky. Stir well. Turn into the tin. Bake in the centre of the oven for 2 ¼ to 2 ½ hours. Leave to cool in the tin. Turn out and remove the paper. If you really must, you can sprinkle more whisky over the cake and brush the top with warmed sieved apricot jam. Cut into portions and wrap.

ENGLISH WEDDING CAKE
9 oz plain flour
1 tsp. ground mixed spice
½ tsp. ground cinnamon
2 ½ lb. mixed fruit
2 oz chopped blanched almonds
3 oz glace cherries
8 oz Demerara sugar
8 oz butter
4 beaten eggs
1 ½ tbs. Black treacle
3 tbs. rum

Method

Sieve together flour and mixed spice in a large bowl. In a separate bowl cream together the butter and sugar until very pale and fluffy. Beat in the eggs, a little at a time, adding a little of the flour to prevent the eggs from curdling. Stir in the treacle and add this to the flour, together with the mixed fruit, peel, cherries and nuts. Stir until well combined. Double line the base and sides of an 8 inch cake tin with grease proof paper. To insulate the tin and prevent the cake burning, tie a band of doubled brown paper around the outside, so that it comes 1 inch above the side of the tin. Turn the cake mixture into the tin and bake in a cool oven at 150°C/300°F/gas mark 2 for 3 hours. Reduce the heat to 140°C/275°F/gas mark 1 and continue cooking for a further 50 minutes or until a skewer inserted comes out clean. Leave the cake in the tin for 10 minutes, during which time it will shrink away from the sides and can then be turned out onto a wire cooling rack. When cool, but not cold, turn the cake upside down and make holes in the bottom with a skewer. Spoon the rum over and allow it to soak in. Leave until cold and wrap and store in an airtight tin. When required, drizzle the cake with a little more rum, over the top this time, coat with marzipan and ice as desired, perhaps with fondant decorations. *The cake should be made six weeks to a month before the event and iced one week before.*

STRAWBERRY ICE CREAM
¾ pt single cream
¼ pt milk
2 oz sugar
Yolks of 3 eggs
½ lb. strawberries

Method

Puree strawberries. Place the cream, milk and sugar in a pan and bring almost to boiling point. Stir in the puree. Reheat again to near boiling point. Remove from heat. Beat the eggs in a clean bowl. Beat in some of the hot cream mixture, then add this to the cream in the pan. Heat gently until the mixture is thick enough to coat the back of a spoon. Cool. Place in the freezer. When it is half frozen, whisk thoroughly and return it to the freezer. After 1 hour, whisk again and do the same after a further hour.

CHOCOLATE AND PEPPERMINT ICE CREAM
4 oz caster sugar
6 oz dark chocolate
2 handfuls chopped peppermint leaves
1 pt double cream
4 eggs separated

Method

Melt 4 oz of the chocolate over a pan of boiling water. Remove from the heat and gradually whisk in the egg yolks. Leave to cool. Meanwhile, whip the cream until stiff, add the chopped peppermint and gradually fold into the chocolate

126

mixture. Put in the freezer until the ice cream begins to set at the edges and whisk again. Return to the freezer for 45 minutes, then whisk once more. Repeat this procedure until the ice cream is completely set. Whisk the egg whites and fold in the caster sugar. Carefully fold this into the frozen ice cream. Return to the freezer until the ice cream is completely set. Serve with mint leaves dipped in chocolate.

STRAWBERRY WATER ICE
3 oz sugar
½ pt water
1 lb. strawberries
1 egg white

Method
Puree the fruit. In a pan, bring the water and sugar to the boil and stir until the sugar dissolves. Allow to cool. Stir in the pureed fruit and pour into freezer trays. Freeze for 30 minutes. Meanwhile whisk the egg white until it forms stiff peaks. Remove the fruit mixture from the freezer and turn out into a bowl. Beat until creamy. Fold in the egg white. Put back in the trays and freeze until set - at least 1 hour.

TRYST
3 oz sugar
½ pt water
Generous handful scented geranium leaves
Few drops lemon oil
1 egg white
A few mint leaves to garnish

Method
In a pan, bring the water, geranium leaves and sugar to the boil and stir until the sugar dissolves. Leave to steep for 1 hour. Remove the leaves, squeezing them to obtain as much flavour as possible and pour the liquid into freezer trays. Freeze for 30 minutes. Meanwhile whisk the egg white until it forms stiff peaks. Remove the mixture from the freezer and turn out into a bowl. Add the lemon oil and beat until creamy. Fold in the egg white. Put back in the trays and freeze until set - at least 1 hour.

SWEETHEARTS
1 lb. icing sugar
¼ lb. cornflour
Evaporated milk

½-1 tsp. strawberry flavouring
Chocolate to coat

Method

Sift together the cornflour and sugar. Stir in the flavouring. Thoroughly mix
in enough evaporated milk to form a stiff but workable paste and knead until
well combined. Turn out onto work top dusted with icing sugar and roll out to
1/8" thick. Cut into heart shapes and leave to dry out thoroughly. Dip in melted
chocolate. Keep in a refrigerator.

HONEY MOON

1 lb. Runny honey
1 cinnamon stick
5 cloves
1 piece bruised root ginger
Grated rind of 1 lemon
½ vanilla pod
2 crushed cardamoms

Method

Put the spices and lemon rind in a jar. Cover with the honey and leave in a dark
cupboard for 3 weeks. Add some to the ritual cup or use to flavour food and
drinks at the handfasting.

VIOLET TWILIGHT

¾ pt single cream
¼ pt milk
2 oz sugar
Yolks of 3 eggs
1 heaped tbs. violet flowers

Method

Place the cream, milk, sugar and flowers in a pan and bring almost to boiling
point. Cover the pan and leave it to stand for 1 hour. Strain the contents
through a sieve or jam bag, pressing the flowers to obtain their flavour. Reheat
the liquid to near boiling point. Remove from the heat. In a bowl beat the eggs.
Beat in some of the hot cream mixture, then add this to the cream in pan. Heat
gently until the mixture is thick enough to coat the back of a spoon. Pour into
a container and leave to cool before placing it in the freezer. When half frozen,
whisk the ice cream thoroughly and return to the freezer. After 1 hour, whisk
again. Leave a further hour and repeat the process. Freeze until ready to serve.

FREYA'S DELIGHT

6 apples, cored

  ½ pt cider
  3 oz dried mixed fruit
  ½ tbs. crushed hazelnuts
  4 oz nuts, shelled and roughly chopped
  2 tbs. medium oats
  3 chopped apricots

Method

Stand the apples in an oven proof dish and fill with the other dried ingredients. Pour the cider around bases of apples and bake in a moderate at 325°F/170°C/ gas mark 3 oven for 40 minutes, until the apples are cooked, basting every ten minutes.

WINES AND ALES

MEAD

  4 lb. honey
  1 orange
  1 lemon
  1 gallon water
  Yeast and nutrient
  Pectic enzyme

Method

Put the water and honey into a pan and bring to the boil. Allow to cool to 21 ° C. Add the juice of the oranges and lemon and add the yeast and nutrient. (A nutrient must be used as modern honey is deficient in important minerals.) Pour into a demi-jon and fit an airlock. Allow to ferment out and bottle. This should be matured for at least a year before drinking if you can possibly resist it that long!

SWEET MEAD

  4 ½ lb. Honey
  Juice of 2 lemons
  Yeast and nutrient
  1 gallon water

Method

Boil half the water with the honey, stirring until the honey has dissolved. Remove from the heat. Allow to cool to 21 ° C. and add the lemon juice and nutrient. Add the rest of the water and transfer to a demi-jon. Add the yeast and fit an airlock.

When a layer of lees settles at the bottom of the jar, rack off into a clean demi-jon. Keep for at least a year before drinking.

HANDFASTING WINE

1 gallon of meadowsweet flowers
1 cup of black tea
1 lb. raisins
Yeast and nutrient
3 lb. White sugar
Juice of 1 lemon
1 gallon water

Method

Put the flowers, chopped raisins and the sugar in a brewing bin. Boil the water and pour over, stir to dissolve the sugar. Add the tea and lemon juice. Cool to 20°C and add the yeast and nutrient. Stand in a warm place for 10 days, stirring twice a day. Strain into a demi-jon and fit an airlock. Bottle when clear.

BRIDE ALE

2 pints water
Piece root ginger
1 ½ lb. honey
Juice of 3 lemons
4 pints cold water
Yeast and nutrient

Method

Boil the 2 pints of water with the ginger for 30 minutes. Meanwhile, put the honey into a brewing bin with the lemon juice and the cold water. Add the boiling water. Allow to cool to 20°C and add the yeast and nutrient. Cover and stand for 24 hours. Strain and bottle. This can be drunk after seven days.

MIXED DRINKS

LOVE TOKEN

2 oz. sloe gin
1 egg white
½ tsp. lemon juice
½ tsp. raspberry juice

Method

Shake all the ingredients well together with crushed ice. Strain into a cocktail glass.

LOVERS' CUP

1 bottle red wine
Juice 1 orange
6 cloves
Juice 1 lemon
3 sticks cinnamon
Brown sugar to taste

Method

Place the wine, fruit juice and spices in a pan and bring slowly to the boil. Simmer gently 5-10 minutes. Remove from the heat and add the sugar to taste, stirring until dissolved. Serve warm.

PLEDGE OF LOVE

1 ½ oz. peach brandy
1 tbs. honey

Method

Stir well in a goblet.

LOVE KNOT

1 ½ oz. blended whisky
1 egg white
1 tsp. lemon juice
½ tsp. powdered sugar
¼ tsp. anise

Method

Shake well with crushed ice. Strain into a cocktail glass.

CHAMPAGNE PUNCH

4 bottles champagne or sparkling wine
1 bottle brandy
1 bottle sherry
1 bottle Madeira wine
4 oz. cherry brandy
1 lb. sugar lumps
2 bottles lemonade
6 sliced oranges
2 sliced lemons
1 pint strawberries

Method

Rub the sugar over the lemons until it has absorbed all the yellow part of the skins of the 6 lemons. Mix the sugar, lemonade and fruits in punch bowl. Add the remaining ingredients and ice. Stir well.

GINGER PUNCH
1 pint tea made with two tea bags
1 pint apple juice
1 pint ginger beer
4 tbs. lemon juice
to decorate:
Lemon slices
Maraschino cherries

Method
Make the tea and remove the tea bags. Add the other liquids, transfer to a punch bowl and decorate with the fruit.

IRISH COFFEE
1 ½ oz. Irish whisky
1 ½ tsp. sugar
Black coffee
Whipped cream

Method
Pour the whisky into a coffee cup. Add the sugar and fill with hot, black coffee. Stir to dissolve sugar. Float whipped cream on top, do not stir. Add a straw if desired.

ATHOLBROSE
1 tsp. clear honey
1 measure whisky

Method
Stir the honey into the whisky and drink. Quantities can be adjusted to taste.
In Scotland, this is considered an ideal breakfast drink!

MULLED WINE
½ lb. brown sugar
½ pint water
12 cloves
Cinnamon stick
½ tsp. ginger powder
1 lemon
1 orange

2 oz raisins
2 bottles red wine
To decorate:
Orange and lemon slices

Method

Put the sugar and water in a pan and heat slowly to dissolve, add the juice of the lemon and orange and their grated rinds and the spices. Boil for five minutes and leave to infuse for an hour. Strain into a large pan, add the raisins and bring to the boil. Add the wine, but do not allow it to boil (all the alcohol disappears!), just warm it through. Serve hot in glasses decorated with orange and lemon slices.

MULLED MEAD

1 pt mead
½ oz bruised ginger
4 cloves
1 cinnamon stick

Method

Heat the mead to no hotter than 60°C with the bruised ginger, cloves cinnamon.

CORIANDER TEA

1 oz coriander herb
1 pint boiling water

Method

Infuse 15 minutes. Strain.
Coriander is a powerful binding herb of love at this time, celebrating both the sacred love of the Lord and Lady and the love of human couples.

MARJORAM TEA

½ pint boiling water
2 tsp. herb

Method

Infuse 15 minutes. Strain.
Marjoram is sacred to the Goddess of Love.

Chapter 12
SPELLS AND LUCKY CHARMS

Because marriage is one of life's great rites of passage, both bride and groom stand on a threshold during the ceremony neither married nor unmarried. This is a moment and state of potential great magical power, which the guests were always keen to tap into, hence all the customs of taking pieces of the bride's dress, her flowers and so on. However, it is also a dangerous position, and for this reason, much wedding magic is concerned with the protection of the bride and groom. While any threshold is powerful, it is also a dangerous place, whether it is not a time, place, or doorway (which is neither inside nor outside, but a boundary between the two- a place between places). When a person crosses a threshold they move from one place or state to another and are in danger from the spirits that dwell *between*. For this reason a bride - in a liminal stage of life- is carried across the threshold into her new house. For the Celts boundaries of any kind were dangerous and gave access to the Otherworld. These included such in between things as a crossroads, the shore between sea and land, midnight, the time between one day and the next and Samhain, the time between one year and the next- or one stage of life and the next.

The character of the wedding is an act of sympathetic magic which sets the tone of the rest of the couple's lives. If it is surrounded by symbols of prosperity and plenty, then this is thought to attract these things later on.

NORDIC PROTECTION POUCH FOR THE GROOM

> 1 x pinch chives, dried
> 1 x pinch rosemary
> 1 x clove garlic
> 1 x iron nail
> Square of blue cloth 3" x 3"
> 1 x 9" length of red thread

Based on a Swedish tradition, this pouch should be secreted about the groom's clothes to protect him from the attentions of jealous forces. It may be prepared by the groom or one of his friends, though not the bride. Take the cloth and sprinkle in the herbs and add the nail, concentrating on the thought of keeping the groom safe on his wedding day and beyond. 'Project' this thought into the herbs, and tie up the pouch with the red thread.

PRE-CEREMONY PURIFICATION BATH

Before the wedding ceremony, you might like to indulge in a purification bath to ensure that you are cleansed, body and soul for what lies ahead.

> 2 handfuls salt
> 2 drops camomile oil (for calm and relaxation)
> 1 drop rosemary oil (for purification)
> 1 drop rose oil (for love)
> 1 drop lime oil (for energy)

Drop the oils into the salt and using a pestle and mortar, blend the oils and salt together. You might like to add colouring, red for love or blue for purification, in the form of a drop of food colouring. Don't overdo this, you don't want to be blue for the ceremony, unless you are having a Pictish wedding complete with woad stains!

LOVE LOCKS

The couple should each cut a lock of each other's hair. This is then placed in a wooden or silver box. This can then be buried in the garden or some site that is special to both. For as long as it endures, they will be linked together.

FIVE ALMONDS

A gift of five almonds represents health, wealth, long life, fertility and happiness.

FOUR FEOHS

A Nordic tradition is to give the couple a gift of four feoh runes, in the form of a carving or painting, or maybe four feohs painted on four stones. They represent flax, fodder, fertility and food.

MEHNDI

In Indian and north Africa the bride is adorned with henna pattern called *mehndi*, which are lucky and protect the bride from evil spirits. The painting is a great occasion shared by her female family and friends.

If you want to decorate your bride, kits containing all you need are readily obtainable, or you can make your own using henna and a couple of other simple ingredients, but please make sure to apply a 'patch test' to make sure the skin is not sensitive to the ingredients.

Wash the area where you wish to apply the design and pat it dry. Mix up the henna powder with water to the consistency of a pancake mix and let it stand for about 30 minutes. Rub a small amount of eucalyptus oil into the skin. You can use a stencil or squeeze applicator to apply the designs. Leave the henna in place for ten minutes until the mixture is dry to the touch. Remove the stencil, if used. Gently brush lemon juice over the design. Wait for a further 30 minutes and apply more lemon juice. Freehand patterns may be formed by gradually building-up the henna with several applications. As it dries, the henna will harden on the skin. The darkness and permanence of the design will depend on your skin type and colour and how long the henna mixture is left in place. Leave in place for 3-24 hours (this may feel 'itchy', see notes on safety), keeping the painted area of skin out of direct sunlight. Remove the hardened henna with water. As a rough guide, mehndi designs can last anything from a couple of days to several weeks.

Mehndi is usually trouble-free but should not be applied to damaged skin, the face (especially near the eyes), or other sensitive areas. If you have allergies or sensitive skin, test the procedure on a small area before applying a large design. Avoid getting the henna on your hands, clothes, furnishings, or anywhere else where you don't want it to stain. If this does happen, wash it off immediately.

ROSEMARY WEDDING WREATH

There is an old eastern European custom of the bride wearing a wreath or chaplet of rosemary, which symbolizes remembrance. The wreath is woven for the bride on the wedding eve by her friends, each making a wish for the bride as they attach a piece of rosemary to the chaplet (for instructions on making wreaths see page?). Each person might say one of the following, or add something of their own:

> *I wish the bride wisdom*
> *I wish the bride loyalty*
> *I wish the bride love*
> *I wish the bride happiness*
> *I wish the bride wealth*
> *I wish the bride health.*

YARROW MARRIAGE CHARM

For a yarrow marriage charm, on a Friday during the waxing moon, take nine dried yarrow flower heads, bind the stems together, add a green ribbon, tie into a bow and hang over the bed. This is given to newly married couples. A bunch over the bed was said to ensure lasting love.

LUCKY HORSESHOE

A lucky horseshoe is given to the bride and groom to keep in their home. English brides carry cardboard horseshoes on their wedding day.

THE BRIDAL BED

It is traditional for the bride's friends to prepare the bridal bed and bedroom for the wedding night. The Greeks think it proper to roll young babies over the bed as a fertility ceremony, while the Chinese encourage young children to sit on it for similar reasons. The bed may be strewn with flowers, seeds, fruits and money, all to ensure fertility and prosperity on all levels. It might be a good idea to put the seeds and fruits in packets as they might be difficult to remove from the sheets. In Greece, young unmarried women also shower the bed with coins, flowers and sugar-coated almond sweets called *koufetta*.

SICILIAN PILLOW CHARM

Two days before the wedding, the mother of the bride puts money under her daughter's pillowcase and the mother of the groom puts money under her son's pillowcase in an act of sympathetic magic to ensure that they will always be prosperous. If you can't get the two mothers to do this, ask two older female members of the coven, or two married friends.

CELTIC LOVE KNOT

This knot symbolises the eternity of love, and Irish brides sometimes embroider it into the handkerchief that they will carry on the day of the wedding. If you want to make one, you can do it as a magical act, reinforcing your love with each embroidery stitch.

BEST MAN SPELL

Based on a Russian custom, the best man can perform a protection spell for the bride by walking three times around her carrying the coven pentacle. The other members of the party shout and bang drums to frighten away negativity. He then kneels in front of her and scratches the ground before her with his athame, declaring that she is protected from anyone who may wish to harm her, human or spirit.

FLORAL PLENTY CHARM

Hide a little bread, salt, sugar, and a coin in the bouquet, or carry these in a small purse to ensure a life that will never want for food or money.

LUCKY BREAK

Greek weddings are characterised by the enthusiastic breaking of plates, symbolising luck.

THIRTEEN COIN SPELL

The Spanish groom gives his bride thirteen golden coins to symbolise his ability to provide for her. The modern Pagan bride may well be the one to present this gift to the groom, but whichever way you do it, place the coins in a small pouch, and hand then over at the conclusion of the ceremony. They are passed back and forth several times, but finish up in the possession of the bride. You could even use chocolate coins in gold paper and eat them afterwards- the symbolism is the same.

Chapter 13
HANDPARTING

With all the best will in the world, relationships sometimes do not work out. The couple may simply go their separate ways, hopefully without recrimination or blame, or choose to undergo a formal handparting ceremony. One partner should not force the other into this, and it should only be done if both parties are on friendly enough terms to undertake it with good will, to bring closure to the relationship, and allow each to move on.

THE HANDPARTING RITUAL

The candles and the altar should be black, which is the colour of Saturn and the colour of endings. One lit black candle, representing the ending relationship, is placed on the altar, flanked by two unlit blue candles for healing. The couple hold the ends of the cord they were originally bound with for the duration of the ceremony, until it is cut by the celebrant. A very sharp knife or shears are placed on the altar for this purpose.

The celebrant cats the circle in the usual manner and announces: *"We are here to mark the handparting of (name) and (name) who wish to separate from each other at this time."*

S/he then addresses the bride: *"(Name) have you come here of your own free will to seek handparting from (name)."*

Bride: *"I have."*

S/he then addresses the groom: *"(Name) have you come here of your own free will to seek handparting from (name)."*

Groom: *"I have."*

Celebrant: *"Then let you be parted without recrimination or blame, neither seeking ill for the other. Remember that this has been one of life's lessons, and youi have learned from your relationship. Cherish the memory of good times you have shared, and relinquish the pain. (Names), are you willing to do so?*

Bride: *"I am."*

Groom: *"I am."*

Celebrant: *"I declare before the Lord and Lady and your brothers and sisters of the Craft, that you are no longer handfast."* S/he cuts the cord they hold between them. *"Let each of you take your own blue candle, which represents the healing journey each of you must now take."* They each light their separate candle from the black central candle, which is them extinguished as a sign that the relationship is finally over. The cords and this candle are burned in the fire, either now or later, by the celebrant.

Celebrant uses the incenses to cleanse the aura of each saying: *"Forget painful thoughts and remember each other kindly."*
Celebrant makes the sign of the pentacle before each with their blue candle: *"Let anger and hatred burn away."*
Celebrant sprinkles each with water saying: *"Be cleansed of heartache and regret."*
Celebrant places a few grains of salt in each of their palms: *"Return to the world and take up your life anew."*

Celebrant: *"The rite is ended. Go in peace."*

The handparted couple then walk to opposite quarters of the circle and exit in different directions.

POEMS AND BLESSINGS FOR HANDFASTINGS

AN IRISH BLESSING

May the flowers always line your path
And sunrise light your day,
May songbirds serenade you,
Every step along the way,
May a rainbow run beside you,
In a sky that's always blue,
And may happiness fill your heart,
Each day your whole life through.

IRISH TOAST

"Friends and relatives, so fond and dear, 'tis our greatest pleasure to have you here. When many years this day has passed, fondest memories will always last. So we drink a cup of Irish mead and ask God's blessing in your hour of need." The guests respond: *"On this special day, our wish to you, the goodness of the old, the best of the new. God bless you both who drink this mead, may it always fill your every need."*

SOME BLESSINGS GUESTS MIGHT LIKE TO USE:

- May your hearts be as warm as your hearthstone.
- May the Gods sleep on your pillow.
- May the Gods be with you and bless you.
- May you see your children's children.
- May you be poor in misfortune, rich in blessings.
- May you know nothing but happiness from this day forward.

LOVE POETRY

You might like to read one of these as part of the ceremony, or at the reception, or adapt part of them for your vows.

Rosin Dubh (Little Black Rose)

Roisin, have no sorrow for all that has
happened to you
the Friars are out on the brine,. they
are travelling the sea
your pardon from the Pope will come,
from Rome in the East
and we won't spare the Spanish wine

for my Roisin Dubh
Far have we journeyed together, since
days gone by.
I've crossed over mountains with her,
and sailed the sea
I have cleared the Erne, though in
spate, at a single leap
and like music of the strings all about
me, my Roisin Dubh
You have driven me mad, fickle girl-
may it do you no good!
My soul is in thrall, not just yesterday
nor today
You have left me weary and weak in
body and mind
O deceive not the one who loves you,
my Roisin Dubh
I would walk in the dew beside you, or
the bitter desert
in hopes I might have your affection,
or part of your love
Fragrant small branch, you have given
your word you love me
the choicest flower of Munster, my
Roisin Dubh
If I had six horses, I would plough
against the hill-
I'd make Roisin Dubh my Gospel in the
middle of Mass-
I'd kiss the young girl who would
grant me her maidenhead
and do deeds behind the lios with my
Roisin Dubh!
The Erne will be strong in flood, the
hills be torn
the ocean will be all red waves, the sky
all blood,
every mountain and bog in Ireland will
shake
one day, before she shall perish, my

Roisin Dubh.
(15th/16th century Irish)

No sickness worse than secret love
It's long, alas, since I pondered that
No more delay; I now confess
my secret love, so slight and slim
I gave a love that I can't conceal
to her hooded hair, her shy intent
her narrow brows, her blue-green eyes
her even teeth and aspect soft
I gave as well - and so declare-
my soul's love to her soft throat
her lovely voice, delicious lips
snowy bosom, pointed breast
And may not overlook, alas,
my cloud-hid love for her body bright
her trim straight foot, her slender sole,
her languid laugh, her timid hand
Allow there was never known before
such a love as mine for her
there lives not, never did, nor will,
one who more gravely stole my love
Do not torment me, lady
Let our purposes agree
You are my spouse on this Fair Plain
so let us embrace
(-anon. 15th/16th century)

Set that berry-coloured mouth
on mine, O skin like foam
Place that smooth and lime-white limb
-despite your quarrel- round me
Slim and delicate, be no longer
absent from my side
Slender, show me to your quilts!
Stretch our bodies side by side
As I have put away (soft thigh)
Ireland's women for your sake

143

likewise try to put away
all other men for me
I gave to your bright teeth
Immeasurable longing
So it is just that you should give
your love in the same measure.

(-**anon**)

She is unique; there is no one like her.
She is more beautiful than any other.
Look, she is like a star goddess rising
At the beginning of a glorious new year;
Brilliantly white, clear skinned;
With beautiful eyes for looking,
With honeyed lips for speaking;
She says not one word too many.
With a long neck and white breast,
Her blue-black hair like lapis lazuli;
Her arm more dazzling than gold;
Her fingers like lotus flowers,
With heavy buttocks and tiny waist.
Her thighs offer her beauty,
as lightly she treads upon ground.
She has captured my heart in her embrace.
Extract from a 3,000 year-old Egyptian papyrus.

Sonnets from the Portuguese

How do I love thee ? Let me count the ways.
I love thee to the depth and breadth and height
My soul can reach, when feeling out of sight
For the ends of Being and ideal Grace.
I love thee to the level of everyday's
Most quiet need, by sun and candle-light.
I love thee freely, as men strive for Right;
I love thee purely, as they turn from Praise.
I love thee with the passion put to use
In my old griefs, and with my childhood's faith.
I love thee with a love I seemed to lose
With my lost saints,—I love thee with the breath,
Smiles, tears, of all my life!—and, if God choose,

I shall but love thee better after death.
Elizabeth Barrett Browning

Sonnet CXVI
Let me not to the marriage of true minds
Admit impediments. Love is not love,
Which alters when it alteration finds,
Or bends with the remover to remove.
Oh, no! it is an ever-fixed mark
That looks on tempests and is never shaken.
It is the star to every wandering bark
Whose worth's unknown, although his height be taken.
Love is not Time's fool, though rosy lips and cheeks
Within his bending sickle's compass come.
Love alters not with his brief hours and weeks,
But bears it out.. even to the edge of doom.
If this be error and upon me proved,
I never writ, nor no man ever loved.
William Shakespeare

Of Pearls and Stars
The pearly treasures of the sea,
The lights that spatter heaven above,
More precious than these wonders are
My heart-of-hearts filled with your love.

The ocean's power, the heavenly sights
Cannot outweigh a love filled heart.
And sparkling stars or glowing pearls
Pale as love flashes, beams and darts.

So, little, youthful maiden come
Into my ample, feverish heart
For heaven and earth and sea and sky
Do melt as love has melt my heart.
Heinrich Heine (1799 - 1856)

My True Love Has My Heart
My true-love hath my heart and I have his,
By just exchange one for the other given;

145

I hold his dear and mine he cannot miss;
There never was a better bargain driven.
My true-love hath my heart and I have his,

His heart in me keeps him and me in one;
My heart in him his thoughts and senses guides;
He loves my heart for once it was his own,
I cherish his because in me it bides.
My true-love hath my heart and I have his.

Philip Sidney (1554 - 1586)

Song: To Celia

Drink to me, only with thine eyes
And I will pledge with mine;
Or leave a kiss but in the cup,
And I'll not look for wine.
The thirst that from the soul doth rise
Doth ask a drink divine:
But might I of Jove's nectar sup
I would not change for thine.

I sent thee late a rosy wreath,
Not so much honouring thee
As giving it a hope that there
It could not withered be
But thou thereon didst only breath
And sent'st it back to me:
Since, when it grows and smells, I swear,
Not of itself but thee.

Ben Jonson (1572 - 1637)

ANNIVERSARIES

First – Cotton. You could make your beloved a present of a new robe, altar cloth or tarot bag.

Second – Paper. How about a good book on magic? Or a blank book for a *Book of Shadows* or *Magical Diary*. Tarot cards would also fall under the heading of 'paper'.

Third – Leather or Straw. Leather might include a leather pouch for ritual equipment, sandals for ritual use, or if you go for straw, a handmade corn dolly would be appropriate.

Fourth – Flowers. Flowers are always acceptable, and you can be as extravagant as you like.

Fifth – Wood. Your lover might appreciate a box to hold ritual tools or tarot cards, an altar fashioned from an antique table or chest, or wood for a wand or staff.

Sixth – Iron or Sugar. Sugar might mean cakes and a celebratory meal together. Iron, on the other hand, might refer to an athame (ritual knife) candlestick, cauldron etc.

Seventh – Wool or Copper. A woollen cloak might be appreciated for those cold winter rituals, or what about a nice copper pentacle for the altar? Copper jewellery and talismans would also be appropriate, especially as it is the metal of Venus.

Eighth – Bronze. A bronze statue of your lover's favourite god or goddess might be a nice anniversary gift.

Ninth – Pottery This might include painted and decorated plates, a ritual cup, small ceramic statuettes or candlesticks.

Tenth – Tin This metal is associated with the Jupiter, the planet of joviality and expansion. Perhaps you could make your beloved a talisman of Jupiter, or simply bring the influence of Jupiter into your lives by taking time to try new things and make new friends. Do something totally different for this anniversary to put some sparkle back into the relationship.

Eleventh – Steel. You needn't interpret this literally, but how about travelling in a steel vehicle, such as a car or train? You could visit a special place, such as a sacred site together.

Twelfth – Silk and Fine Linen This might be silken robe or new cord handmade from silken threads.

Thirteenth – Lace An altar cloth with lace edging would be a nice ritual present, or a special gift on a lace cushion could be fun.

Fourteenth – Ivory. Real ivory is not very environmentally friendly or ethical, so unless you can find an antique piece, stick to ivory coloured items. This could include flowers, clothing, pottery or jewellery.

Fifteenth – Crystal Crystals of all kinds would be suitable, maybe a healing crystal wand, a crystal pendant or earrings, a dowsing crystal and so on.

Twentieth – China This might include painted and decorated plates, a ritual cup, small ceramic statuettes or candlesticks.

Twenty-fifth – Silver. Silver jewellery, pentacles or cloak pins are suitable, as is a silver chalice. Silver is also the colour of the moon, and you might buy moon shaped jewellery, plates or linen with moon patterns.

Thirtieth – Pearl This needn't mean pearl jewellery, but could be pearl coloured flowers or clothes or pottery with a pearlised glaze.

Thirty-fifth – Coral. Again, coral is not very environmentally friendly or ethical, so unless you can find an old piece, stick to coral coloured items, or maybe go with a sea theme? Both are sacred to the Goddess of Love after all.

Fortieth – Ruby. You might give your beloved jewellery, cufflinks or a tie pin with a real ruby, or go with a ruby coloured theme, and buy ruby coloured goblets, flowers or clothes.

Forty-fifth – Sapphire Again, you could buy something with real sapphires, or go with sapphire coloured flowers, glassware, or pottery, etc.

Fiftieth – Golden This is the metal of the sun and of the Sun God. Use it to bring some of his vital energy into your lives with gifts of gold rings or chains, or simply sun symbols, mobiles and hangings.

Fifty-fifth – Emerald If you don't want to buy real emeralds, how about a trip to somewhere green, like the Emerald Isle (Ireland)? Or buy something eco-friendly that helps the environment.

Sixtieth – Diamond The diamond is reputedly made from the flames of love, and sixty years together means that your love must be very strong and enduring. It could be the occasion of a family celebration, or you might like to spend it alone together over a quiet dinner. A diamond ring or pin would be a lovely gift.

RESOURCES

THE BEACON
http://the-beacon.org.uk
Handfasting and marriage ceremonies which can be tailored to constitute a civil marriage.

GREENER WEDDINGS ADVICE http://www.direct.gov.uk/en/
Environmentandgreenerliving/Greenerlifeevents

UK GOVERNMENT ADVICE ON MARRIAGE: http://www.
direct.gov.uk/en/Governmentcitizensandrights/Registeringlifeevents/
Marriagesandcivilpartnerships

FINDING YOUR LOCAL REGISTER OFFICE IN THE UK
http://maps.direct.gov.uk

THE PAGAN FEDERATION
BM Box 7097,
London
WC1N 3XX
UK

LIFERITES (provides list of celebrants willing to officiate)
PO Box 101
Aldershot
GU11 3UN
UK

Odinshof
BCM Tercel
London
WC1N 3XX
UK

ORDER OF BARDS, OVATES AND DRUIDS
PO Box 1333
Lewes
East Sussex
BM7 7ZG
UK

PAGAN ALLIANCE INC
PO Box 666
Williamstown
VIC 3016
Australia

AR NDRAIOCHT FEIN
American Druid Order
PO Box 516
E. Syracuse
NY 13057
USA

INTERNATIONAL GAY AND LESBIAN PAGAN COALITION
PO Box 26442
Oklahoma City
OK 73126 0442
USA

NORDIC PAGAN FEDERATION
PO Box 1814
Bergen
Norway

SACRI RADICI
Co 54 Forli Centro
47100 Forli
Italy

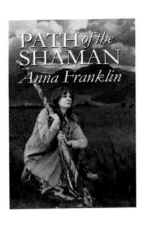

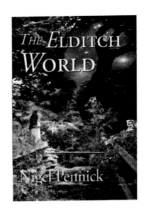

THE PATH OF THE SHAMAN

Anna Franklin

The Path of the Shaman is book two in Anna Franklin's *Eight Paths of Magic* series, exploring the role of the shaman, the mediator between the world of humankind and the world of spirits. This book explores, from the perspective of native British shamanism, the shamanic cosmos, the web of power, the shamanic crisis and becoming a shaman, healing and soul work, as well as working with the spirits of the land, plus animal and plant allies.

"I was moved beyond words by the beginning of this book. It reminded me of my traumatic numinous experiences which I have studiously tried to forget. It woke in me those vestiges of that path which I did not wish to traverse. I learned more, understood more and recognized more than I had before."
New Moon Reviews

£12.95 ISBN 978-0-9547534-4-3

THE ELDRITCH WORLD

Nigel Pennick

The Eldritch World is a place redolent of the quality of strangeness and wonder with a seeming immunity to the passing of time; a place where there is no separation of humans and animals, and humans have the power of understanding the language of birds and beasts. Here, we shall walk the trackways of the mythological landscapes where we may encounter the malign and beneficent, the archaic and the arcane, the masked and the spectral, the formless, faceless and nameless. We shall visit the Weird Lady of the Woods, hide with King Charles in the Royal Oak and frequent the crossroads under the raven wings of night. Dare you take the first step on a journey from which there may be no return?

"Few books have been written specifically about the Otherworld...very highly recommended."
Michael Howard, The Cauldron Magazine

£10.95 ISBN 978-0-9547534-3-6

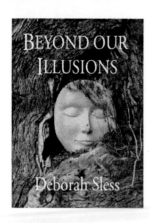

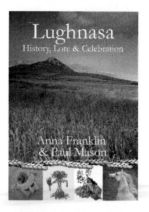

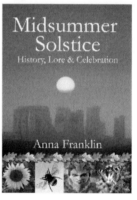

BEYOND OUR ILLUSIONS
Deborah Sless

"As you believe so it becomes" is the Law of Belief, one of the Universal Laws. These Laws have their origins in many philosophies. Once we learn how to work with the Universal Laws we can bring into our lives the things we want. Beyond Our Illusions explores and defines the workings of the Master Law of Cause and Effect and its sub-laws, the Laws of Nature, the Laws of Self and the Law of Transformation. It describes how the reader's psychological make-up can actually prevent these Laws from working in the ways that they expect. The author uses her extensive psychotherapeutic training and experience to help the reader enter their psyche and gain an insight into their inner world that influences the outcome of the Universal Laws.

£11.95, ISBN 978-0-9547534-7-4

BUY ONLINE!

FOR A FULL LIST OF ALL LEAR BOOKS AND SPECIAL OFFERS, VISIT WWW.LEARBOOKS.CO.UK